Penguin F
The Pengu

Colin McEvedy is the author of
The Penguin Atlas of Ancient History,
The New Penguin Atlas of Medieval
History, The Penguin Atlas of Modern
History, The Penguin Atlas of North
American History, The Penguin Atlas
of Recent History and the *Century*
World History Factfinder. He is also
co-author of *The Atlas of World*
Population History with Richard
Jones (Penguin).

Colin McEvedy

THE PENGUIN ATLAS OF AFRICAN HISTORY

Penguin Books

PENGUIN BOOKS

Published by the Penguin Group
Penguin Books Ltd, 27 Wrights Lane, London W8 5TZ, England
Penguin Books USA Inc., 375 Hudson Street, New York, New York 10014, USA
Penguin Books Australia Ltd, Ringwood, Victoria, Australia
Penguin Books Canada Ltd, 10 Alcorn Avenue, Toronto, Ontario, Canada M4V 3B2
Penguin Books (NZ) Ltd, 182–190 Wairau Road, Auckland 10, New Zealand

Penguin Books Ltd, Registered Offices: Harmondsworth, Middlesex, England

First published by 1980
Published simultaneously by Allen Lane
10 9 8

Printed in Hong Kong

Set in Monophoto Apollo by
Filmtype Sevices Limited, Scarborough
Designed by Keith Burns

Contents

Introduction

This atlas consists of fifty-nine maps of Africa covering the period from 175 million years ago to AD 2000, together with an explanatory text. The maps always cover the same area of the globe, which means that once the other continents have moved off and the climate has settled down they show the same geographical outline every time. The central feature of this is, of course, Africa, but besides Africa the base map includes the southern part of Europe and the south-western part of Asia: it does not include Mauritius, Réunion and the Seychelles, islands that geographers traditionally associate with Africa but which lie beyond the right-hand edge of the projection used here; nor is the history of these islands covered in the accompanying text.

At present – a phrase that, as far as this book goes, means mid-1978 – mainland Africa contains forty-five sovereign states. Near-by islands – the Cape Verde group, São Tomé and Principe, Madagascar and the Comoros – provide four more

and the overall total will rise to fifty when Namibia becomes independent in 1979. This is a considerably higher number than any of the other continents – Europe, for example, contains only thirty – and Africa currently provides political geographers with more excitement than all the rest put together. Putting this situation in its historical context is one of the main purposes of this book.

What it is not intended to be is a reference atlas. The maps show only the bare essentials of African geography; the text contains no more facts than are needed to sustain the narrative. If you know what you are looking for and it is in the book you should be able to find it either directly – the book is organized in a simple, chronological way – or by using the index. But it is not a compendium, it's an outline, as indeed it has to be if it is to cover the whole story of man in Africa. Which is really what the book is about.

ONE hundred and seventy-five million years ago the continents that constitute the earth's land mass were all grouped together in one huge super-continent, Pangaea. Africa was in the middle of this conglomerate, in fact its north-western bulge formed the connection between Pangaea's two lobes, Laurasia (which consisted of North America, Europe and northern Asia) and Gondwanaland (South America, Africa, southern Asia, Antarctica and Australia). Because of this land bridge successful animals like the first important mammalian group, the marsupials, were able to spread to every corner of the earth: this became much more difficult after Pangaea began to break up, a process that started some 160 million years ago.

175 million years ago

THE first part of Pangaea to break away consisted of Antarctica and Australia, which began to move off together about 160 million years ago. They bore with them a marsupial population typical of the era. The rest of the continent stayed together, though not without some ominously widening cracks, for another 50 million years, during which time a new group of mammals, the placentals, evolved. The placentals were more efficient than the marsupials and entirely replaced them in most parts of the world. Australia they couldn't get at, however, which is why there is still a thriving marsupial fauna there today.

One class of early placentals that is of particular importance is the group called *prosimii*. As the name implies prosimians are the stock from which the monkeys developed and so are the ultimate ancestors of apes and men. When the next break away from Gondwanaland occurred, the splitting-off of Madagascar by the formation of the Mozambique channel, the prosimians known as lemurs represented the last word in this line of development: as a result Madagascar has lemurs like Australia has marsupials — and no monkeys at all.

South America was the next to go. By then monkeys of a sort were in existence and in the ninety million years since then South America's have evolved into the *platyrrhine* order (marmosets, spider-monkeys etc.) characteristic of the new world. In the old world monkey evolution was to follow a different and more fruitful path with the development of the *catarrhine* order (macaques, baboons etc.) as the first step.

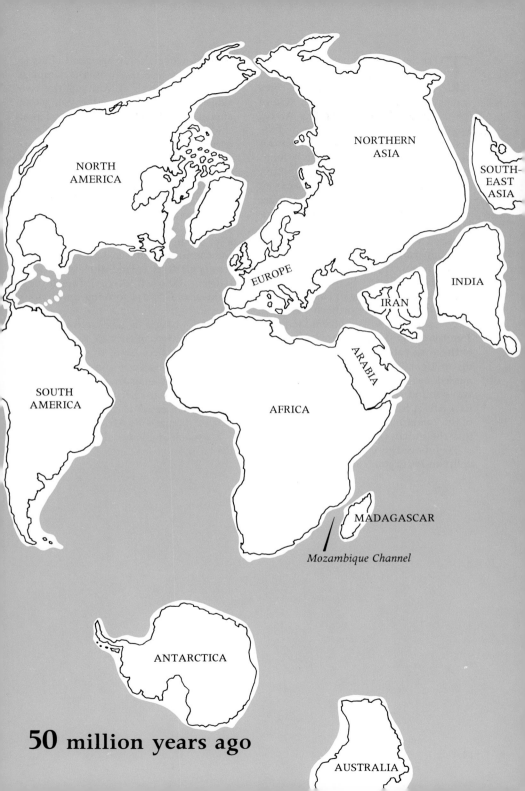

NORTH
AMERICA

NORTHERN
ASIA

SOUTH-
EAST
ASIA

EUROPE

INDIA

IRAN

ARABIA

SOUTH
AMERICA

AFRICA

MADAGASCAR

Mozambique Channel

ANTARCTICA

50 million years ago

AUSTRALIA

THE last major episode of crustal splitting involving Africa started five million years ago when three cracks appeared on the eastern side of the continent. One crack broke Arabia away, creating the Gulf of Aden and the Red Sea and reducing the area of contact between Africa and Asia to the Isthmus of Suez. The two other cracks didn't open up to anything like the same extent – at least they haven't so far – and are visible today as 'rift valleys', straight-sided trenches averaging thirty miles across. The eastern rift starts at the Gulf of Aden, runs south-west through the middle of the Abyssinian massif, turns south at the Ethiopia–Kenya border and, after passing to the east of Lake Victoria, finally peters out in northern Tanzania. The western rift runs up from the lower Zambesi towards Lake Victoria but shifts to the west before it gets there and ends up in Uganda. If the two rifts hadn't missed each other by going opposite ways round Lake Victoria the whole of East Africa from the Horn to the mouth of the Zambesi might well be floating off into the Indian Ocean by now.

To follow the exact course of these splits and rifts you really need geological data. However, there are good clues to where they are on even the simplest map. For example if you put the two sides of the Red Sea together you get an almost exact fit. There is an overlap at the bottom which geologists will tell you corresponds to the Afar Triangle, an area on the south coast which has been filled in relatively recently by lava flows: otherwise the match is perfect. The clues to the rift valleys are the lakes that lie in their floors. The ones in the east valley are, with the exception of Lake Turkana, a bit on the small side and need looking for carefully. But the sequence in the western rift is splendidly clear, Lakes Albert, Edward, Kivu, Tanganyika, Rukwa and Nyasa forming an obvious chain.

Lake Victoria is also related to the rifts. The edges of rifts are pushed up as well as out: because of this the overlap between the eastern and western rifts encloses a saucer-shaped depression. Lake Victoria is really just a big puddle that has collected at the bottom of this: despite its size – it's Africa's biggest lake – it's much shallower than the lakes in the rifts.

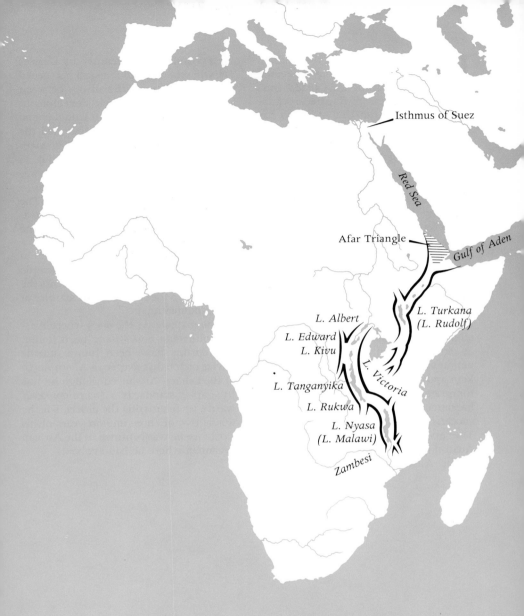

Isthmus of Suez

Red Sea

Afar Triangle

Gulf of Aden

L. Albert

L. Edward
L. Kivu

L. Turkana
(L. Rudolf)

L. Victoria

L. Tanganyika

L. Rukwa

L. Nyasa
(L. Malawi)

Zambesi

3 million years ago

FOR much of the last two million years vast icecaps have covered northern Europe and Canada. During these Ice Ages the climate in southern Europe and the United States has been cold and dry. In Africa it wasn't so much colder than now, but it was dryer. The Sahara Desert became an almost impassable barrier for land animals, while south of it the area of forest contracted to its present limits. Open grassland with isolated trees became the characteristic landscape in the east and south of the continent.

As the forest contracted – a process that probably began about five million years ago – so did the range of the monkeys and apes. Both had evolved in the trees, and though the biggest apes had become too heavy to do much climbing they remained forest browsers as closely tied to this environment as monkeys. However, one class of monkeys and one class of apes did move on to the grasslands. The monkeys were the baboons, who became one of the most successful orders in the monkey world. The apes were the ancestors of the Australopithecines.

The Australopithecines are the ape men postulated last century by Charles Darwin when he put forward his theory of evolution: they are halfway between apes and men. But their development was far from even: in fact it would not be too misleading to say that they had the brains of apes and the bodies of men. When you think of it this is not so surprising. The challenge of the savannah, the grassland environment, was to find a new style of locomotion. The baboons went quadrupedal, the Australopithecines bipedal. As a result the Australopithecines' hands were free for other functions. They soon put them to good use, chipping pebbles into simple cutting instruments. This represents the first stage in the characteristic activity of man, toolmaking.

The map shows the sites where Australopithecine bones have been found. No remains have been found outside Africa or for that matter in Africa north of the Sahara. Advanced though he was by ape standards *Australopithecus* wasn't up to crossing the desert. For the whole two or three million years of his existence he was confined to the African savannah where he had evolved.

SAHARA

FOREST
ZONE

Awash valley

Omo river

L. Turkana
(L. Rudolf)

L. Baringo

Olduvai gorge,
Peninj,
Garusi

KALAHARI

Makapan

Swartkrans,
Sterkfontein,
Kromdraai

Taung

◉ Australopithecine sites

1.5 million years ago

BY one million years ago men of a primitive sort – *Homo erectus* as opposed to *Homo sapiens* – had evolved from the Australopithecines of sub-Saharan Africa. *Homo erectus* had a brain half as big again as *Australopithecus*: he knew how to make fire; he produced flint instruments with an elegant symmetrical finish and (we can be pretty sure of this because of the close association between dexterity and speech) he could talk. These abilities not only put him in a different class from *Australopithecus* biologically, they put him in a different class competitively. Before very long the Australopithecines disappeared – either through direct slaughter or because they had been pushed off their range into areas where they couldn't survive.

Homo erectus also proved bright enough to break through the Saharan barrier, presumably by moving down the Nile valley. As a result he was able to spread across the whole of the Old World: his bones have been found in Europe (near Heidelberg), China (near Peking) and Indonesia (in Java), as well as in North Africa (at Casablanca, Rabat and Ternifine). Only the Americas and Oceania remained beyond his reach.

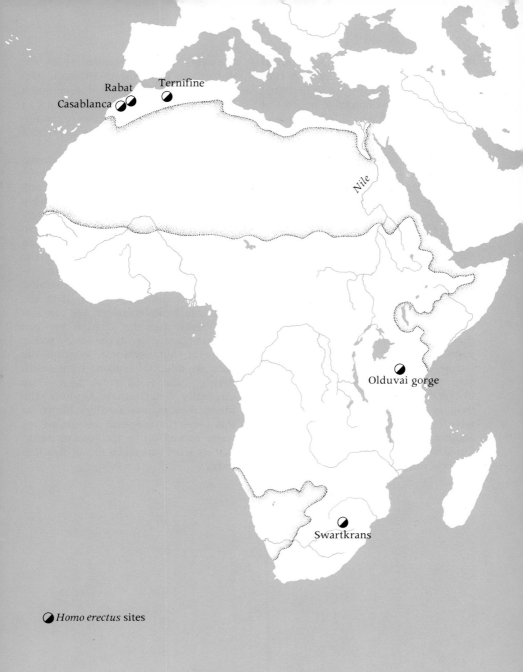

Rabat

Casablanca

Ternifine

Nile

Olduvai gorge

Swartkrans

● *Homo erectus* sites

0.5 million years ago

BY the time the last Ice Age reached its final peak men of modern type (*Homo sapiens*) were to be found throughout the habitable parts of Europe, Asia and Africa. They weren't quite the same as us: they had heavier brows and jaws and less chin but they had brains as big as ours and are better regarded as a variety of modern man than as a separate species.

Men of this type are called Neanderthalers, after the place in Germany where a skull of one was found in 1856: the first skull of the sort from sub-Saharan Africa didn't come to light till 1921, when one was found at the Broken Hill mine in Zambia. This 'Rhodesian man' (Zambia at this time was known as Northern Rhodesia) differs in some minor respects from the standard Neanderthal man. Of course there is considerable variation among Neanderthalers from Europe and one skull isn't enough to start generalizing about, but in this instance the anthropologists who thought the peculiarities significant were proved right: twenty years later another skull of 'Rhodesian man' was found at Saldanha Bay, near Capetown. The other sub-Saharan finds have unfortunately been too fragmentary or too dubious to make the distribution map entirely convincing, but it very much looks as if the Neanderthalers living in Africa south of the Sahara were racially distinct from the Neanderthalers of Europe and North Africa.

There is nothing really surprising about this because populations always do vary from one climate to another and Europe and Africa could hardly have had more different climates than they did during the last Ice Age. We can reasonably postulate that 'Rhodesian man' was darker (because pigment in the skin protects it from the damaging effects of sunlight) and less hairy (because hair slows down heat loss) than the European Neanderthalers. We can also confidently put the division between the two populations at the Sahara rather than the Mediterranean because the only Neanderthal remains from North Africa — the Haua Fteah find — are classically Neanderthal. Anyhow, the Mediterranean was hardly a barrier at this time: the immense amount of sea water locked up in the icecaps meant that its level was much lower than it is today.

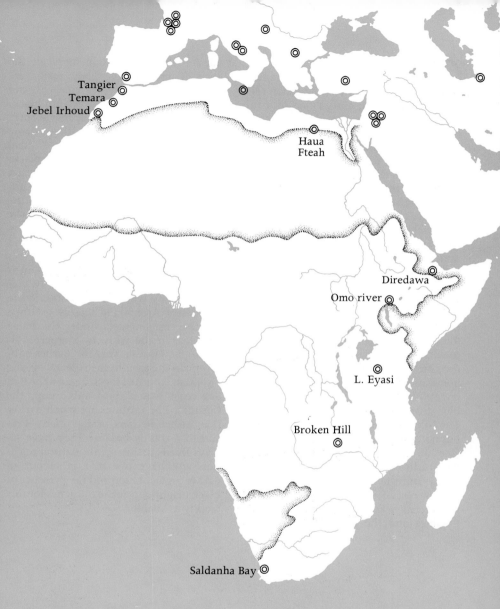

Tangier
Temara
Jebel Irhoud

Haua
Fteah

Diredawa

Omo river

L. Eyasi

Broken Hill

Saldanha Bay

◎ *Homo sapiens* sites

40,000 BC

ONLY a few new genes were needed to change Neanderthalers and their Rhodesian relatives into contemporary types of man, and wherever it was that the new genes first appeared they had spread through the entire human stock before the last Ice Age came to an end. Heavy brow ridges vanished from Africa as completely as they did from Europe and Asia: all the varieties of man known today are classified within the same subspecies, i.e. as *Homo sapiens* var. *sapiens*.

Not that this means all men are the same; every continent has one or more easily distinguishable races. Africa has a particularly large number, five in all, and we can be sure that four of them differentiated there because until comparatively recently they were to be found nowhere else. They are the Negroes, the Nilo-Saharans, the Pygmies and the Bushmen. The Negroes' original homeland was the forest and bush country of West Africa: they were, and are, big, black-skinned and broad-nosed. The Nilo-Saharans are also big and black but noticeably thinner in both body and face: at this time they were probably confined to the middle third of the Nile valley and the area immediately round it. The rest of sub-Saharan Africa (bar the Horn) was divided between the Pygmies and the Bushmen. The Pygmies' habitat is the rain forest of the Zaire (Congo) basin. They really are small, averaging only 4 ft 6 ins. (137 cm) in height: their skin is brown to black, their noses broad and their hair scanty. The Bushmen are bigger without being big (average height 5 ft 2 ins., 157 cm) and yellow rather than brown or black: the hair of their heads grows in tufts that give it a characteristic 'peppercorn' look. Now they are confined to the Kalahari Desert in the south-west of the continent but at the time we are talking of they had the whole of eastern and southern Africa to themselves.

Africa north of the Sahara was then as now a quite different world. It was inhabited by white races related to the Semites of Arabia and loosely grouped together by linguists under the name Hamites. In the west, in Morocco, Algeria and Tunisia, was the Berber subgroup; in the east, in the Nile valley, the Egyptian. South of the Sahara on the Red Sea coast was a third sub-group, the Cushitic. The Cushites are much darker than either Berbers or Egyptians. Presumably this is because they have always lived further south: natural selection will have operated in favour of darker pigmentation and the presence of black neighbours made the genes for this readily available.

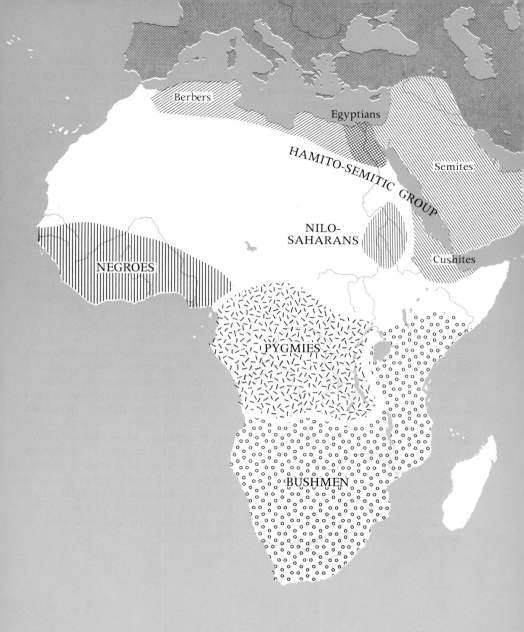

Berbers

Egyptians

HAMITO-SEMITIC GROUP

Semites

NILO-
SAHARANS

Cushites

NEGROES

PYGMIES

BUSHMEN

8000 BC

DURING the palaeolithic and mesolithic eras, the Old and Middle Stone Ages, man subsisted entirely by food gathering: by hunting and fishing, by picking fruits and digging for roots. The hallmark of the neolithic, the New Stone Age, is the shift to food producing: to sowing and reaping edible plants and to tending and herding domesticated animals. The changeover began in the Near East, where the cultivation of wheat and barley and the domestication of sheep, goats, pigs and cattle became established techniques in the course of the seventh millennium. In consequence numbers began to increase, at first slowly and then more rapidly.

Most of the communities that went in for the type of mixed farming characteristic of this period were entirely sedentary: they lived in permanent villages which even as early as this were sometimes walled. Others concentrated more on the herding aspect, driving their animals to different pastures at different seasons. Mobility became their leading characteristic. Thus began the dichotomy between nomad and peasant, between the inhabitants of the steppe (which is good for nothing else but grazing) and the settled, ultimately urban, society which was to generate nearly all the population increase.

Africa played no part at all in these developments: indeed it remained completely unaffected by them until about 5000 BC. Then finally the new techniques were successfully transferred from the valley of the Jordan to the valley of the Nile, from Palestine to Egypt. From there there was a further slow spread along the Mediterranean coast to the Maghreb (Tunisia, Algeria, Morocco) and up the Nile to the Sudan (by 3000 BC). The last stage (as far as this map is concerned) came with the relatively rapid surge of pastoralists from the Sudan westward through the Sahel corridor, the belt of steppe country immediately south of the Sahara Desert.

If the neolithic revolution took a long time to get to Africa and made only slow progress there even after it had, it did have spectacular success at its point of entry, Egypt. The Egyptians quickly learned how to use the seasonal flooding of the Nile to irrigate their crops: as a result their numbers rose to the point where Egypt – the habitable part, that is – became the most densely populated country in the world. This is the economic background to an undoubted African first, the creation of the world's first sizable state. In or around 3000 BC King Menes of Upper Egypt (meaning up-river or southern Egypt) defeated his rivals in Lower Egypt (the north, the Nile delta) and became sole king or pharaoh.

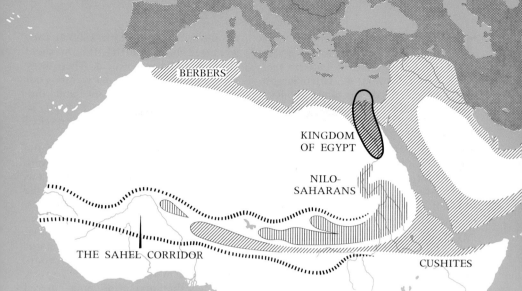

BERBERS

KINGDOM
OF EGYPT

NILO-
SAHARANS

THE SAHEL CORRIDOR

CUSHITES

2750 BC

EGYPT remained the world's most important kingdom for an amazingly long time: it had no real rivals at all until 2300 BC, when Sargon the Great united Mesopotamia (modern Iraq), and a thousand years after that there were still only three major powers in existence: the Egyptian empire (which now included Palestine), the Babylonian empire (which had succeeded Sargon's in Mesopotamia) and the Hittite empire (centred on the eastern half of Turkey). Of the three undoubtedly the most impressive was Egypt: it had an air of having been there forever that the others couldn't match.

The ancient Egyptians put the upriver (southern) limit of their country at the point where the Nile first ceases to be navigable, the rock-strewn gorge at Aswan known as the first cataract. Beyond lay the country that they called Cush and we call Nubia. Around 2000 BC Egyptian troops occupied Nubia as far as the second cataract and in 1500 BC they advanced to the fourth — the threshold of the sub-Saharan world. There they stopped. The new province was too poor to support a further advance and communications with Egypt were already so tenuous they could hardly be stretched further.

The tribes immediately south of the Egyptians were Nilo-Saharans, as were those in the Sahel corridor as far west as Lake Chad. Between Lake Chad and the middle Niger were the Chadic peoples, who relate to the Cushites but have been cut off from them for so long now that they are given independent status within the Hamitic language group. South-west of them were the Negroes. The neolithic revolution now entered their zone, the West African bush country, the emphasis changing back from pastoralism to agriculture (particularly the growing of sorghum) as it did so.

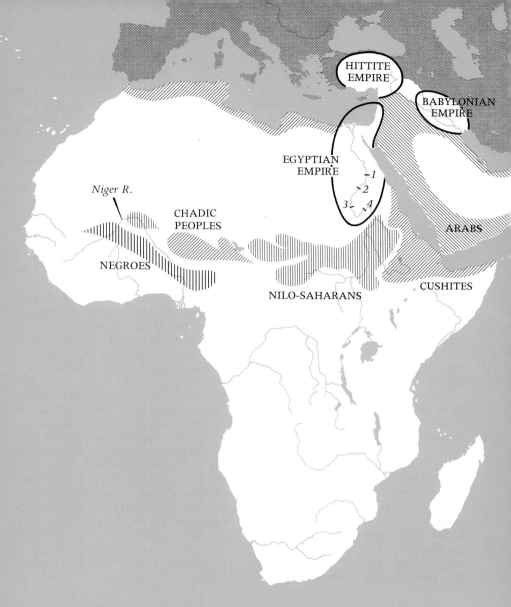

HITTITE EMPIRE

BABYLONIAN EMPIRE

EGYPTIAN EMPIRE

Niger R.

CHADIC PEOPLES

NEGROES

NILO-SAHARANS

ARABS

CUSHITES

1, 2, 3, 4   Nile cataracts

1250 BC

THE Egyptians lost control of Nubia around 1000 BC and we have no record of what went on there for the next 200 years. Then, in the early eighth century BC, Nubia reappears on the map in the form of an independent state with kings powerful enough to wrest Upper Egypt from the feeble pharaohs of the twenty-fourth dynasty. At the same time the Nubians advanced their southern frontier, finally reaching a line well to the south of the confluence of the White and Blue Niles. The zenith of this Nubian kingdom was reached under King Piankhy (751–716 BC), who conquered Lower Egypt and became in consequence first pharaoh of Egypt's twenty-fifth dynasty.

The new dynasty was not a long-lived one. One of Piankhy's sons, Taharqa (688–663 BC), unwisely provoked the all-conquering Assyrians, who throughout this period were masters of most of the Near East. They sent an army that ran the Nubians out of Egypt in no time at all. After that the Nubian kings stayed at home, never appearing north of the second cataract again.

Very few Near Eastern states did any better than this against the Assyrians: one that did was the Phoenician trading city of Tyre. It was able to hold out because of its situation (it was built on a small island off the Lebanese coast) and its fleet (which was the most powerful in the Mediterranean): the Assyrian army simply couldn't get at it. Economically the Tyrians' special secret was their discovery of Spain and its silver mines: they took great care to protect this route, planting colonies on either side of the Tunisian–Sicilian narrows to stop their rivals using it. By the date of this map several of the colonies on the Tunisian side – particularly Carthage and Utica – had grown into cities almost as rich and powerful as Tyre itself. They are important in African history because they introduced the arts of civilization – intensive agriculture, metal working, writing – to this corner of the continent and because, under Carthaginian leadership, they eventually broke away from Tyre and founded an empire of their own.

Metallurgical skills are the simplest measure of technical progress, which is why the first classification archaeologists developed was the Stone Age–Bronze Age–Iron Age one. The Bronze Age isn't of much importance in Africa because only Egypt (from 3000 BC) and Nubia (from 1500 BC) ever had Bronze Ages at all: the rest of the continent was still in the Stone Age when the Assyrians introduced iron. This map, then, marks the formal end of the continent's restricted Bronze Age and the beginning of its Iron Age. Just as important however are changes in the. Stone Age zone. In the Abyssinian highlands and in West Africa food producers appeared among the food gatherers: both these areas now enter the phase of population growth that is associated with this changeover.

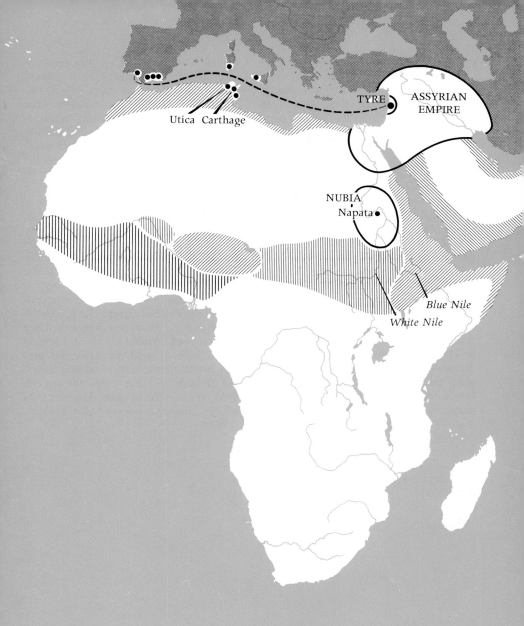

Utica Carthage

TYRE

ASSYRIAN
EMPIRE

NUBIA
Napata

Blue Nile

White Nile

660 BC

THE Assyrian empire was eventually succeeded by the even bigger Persian empire, which stretched across the whole Near East from Europe to India. Its African part, conquered in 525 BC by the half-mad King Cambyses, included Cyrenaica as well as Egypt. Cambyses also attempted to annex Nubia, but this expedition was a failure, only worth a mention because it possibly provoked the transfer of Nubia's seat of government from Napata to Meroe: the frontier between Nubia and Egypt remained as before, at the second cataract.

Cyrenaica takes its name from Cyrene, a city founded by the Greeks sometime around 625 BC. Persian suzerainty didn't stop the Greeks founding more cities in the area and by the second century BC there were five of them: that is why an alternative classical name for the area is the Libyan Pentapolis. The other maritime province of present-day Libya received three Phoenician colonies, which is why it was (and still is) called Tripolitania. In neither instance did the city dwellers or their distant suzerains succeed in imposing themselves on the scattered pastoralists of the hinterland. This split between intrusive, civilized, city-oriented agriculturalists on the coast and indigenous 'barbarian' pastoralists in the interior was to become characteristic of North Africa west of Egypt.

The Carthaginians were not the only Semitic people to colonize Africa: at some time near the date of this map several Arabian tribes crossed the Red Sea and settled in Eritrea. They quickly established themselves as masters of the local Cushites: in doing so they drove a wedge between the other Cushitic peoples of the Red Sea littoral, the Beja to the north and the Danakil to the south. They also moved inland with surprising speed: indeed the Abyssinian massif gets its name from one of these Semitic tribes, the Habesh. A sister tribe, the Ag'azi, were eventually to give Abyssinia its official language, known today as Geez.

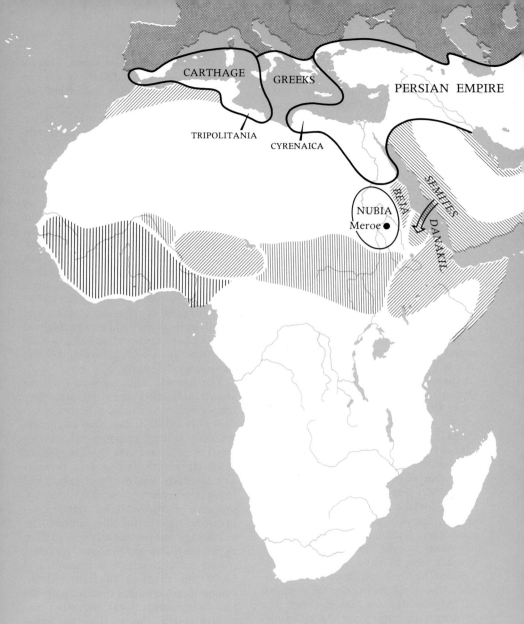

CARTHAGE GREEKS PERSIAN EMPIRE

TRIPOLITANIA

CYRENAICA

NUBIA
Meroe

BEJA

SEMITES

DANAKIL

500 BC

BETWEEN 334 and 325 BC Alexander the Great, king of Macedon in Greece, conquered the Persian empire. Egypt fell without fighting and his visit there (in the winter of 332–1) was short. It was, however, sufficient for him to mark out the site of a new capital for the country – Alexandria, on the Canopic branch of the Nile – and to take a trip into the Libyan desert to the shrine of Zeus-Ammon at the oasis of Siwa. The god greeted him as a son, which was sensible of him: Alexander had already done well and was set to do even better.

After Alexander's death in 323 Egypt became the fief – eventually the kingdom – of one of his generals, Ptolemy. Most of the rest of the empire was acquired by another general, Seleucus. The dynasties these two founded lasted a long time, for much of which they squabbled ineffectively over Palestine. A much more serious conflict developed at the other end of the Mediterranean. There Carthage and Rome fought bitterly for what amounted to the hegemony of the classical world. In 202, at Zama in Tunisia, the struggle reached its climax: two Roman legions supported by Numidian cavalry squared off against the main Carthaginian army with its eighty war elephants.

The Indians were the first people to use elephants in battle: the Greeks first encountered them during Alexander's invasion of the Punjab. Alexander doesn't seem to have been greatly impressed by their performance but Seleucus was and eventually he swapped off Afghanistan for 500 of them. The Ptolemies countered with African elephants which they got from Nubia or,

via the Adulis–Berenice route, Eritrea: they were small and relatively easy to tame, which the bigger ones from further south are not. The elephants the Carthaginians used were a local North African breed that doesn't exist any more: it was hunted out during the Roman period.

Of all the generals who used elephants Hannibal the Carthaginian is undoubtedly the most famous. This is largely because he took a number with him when he marched to Italy at the beginning of the second Roman–Carthaginian war (218 BC). Actually he lost most of these crossing the Alps and they don't figure much in his battles there. Only after he came back to Africa did he get another lot of elephants together and for all the good they did him he might as well not have bothered: at Zama, for the first time in his long career, he was completely defeated.

The Romans didn't annex Carthage immediately after their victory, they simply enlarged the new Berber kingdom of Numidia at Carthage's expense. Another Berber kingdom which emerged at this time was the kingdom of Mauretania with its centre in present-day Morocco. South of the Sahara the important event to note is the appearance of iron-working communities in central Nigeria (the Nok culture). The technology had presumably spread from Egypt via Nubia and the Sahel corridor: spread from North Africa seems less likely (for the lack of trans-Saharan communication at this time see page 38) and independent local invention improbable (the timing fits the transmission hypothesis too well).

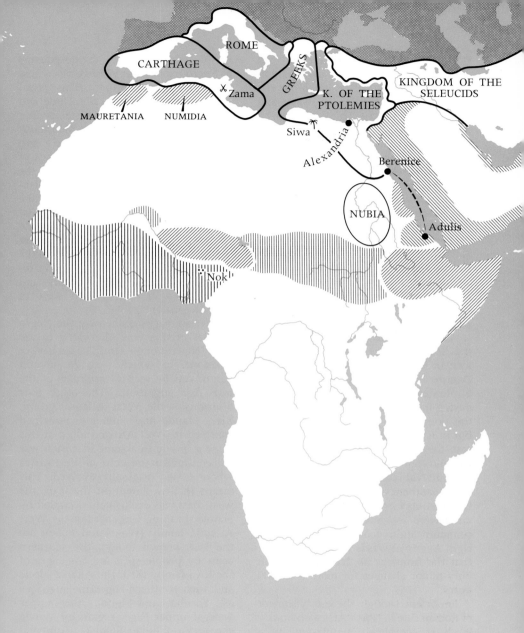

ROME

CARTHAGE

MAURETANIA   NUMIDIA

✕ Zama

GREEKS

K. OF THE
PTOLEMIES

KINGDOM OF THE
SELEUCIDS

Siwa

Alexandria

Berenice

NUBIA

Adulis

Nok

202 BC

THE third and final war between Rome and Carthage was fought in 149–146 BC, after which the victorious Romans laid the city waste and annexed its territory. This gave them an African province roughly equivalent to the northern half of Tunisia. Over the next two centuries they took over the rest of North Africa: Cyrenaica in 74 BC, Numidia in two bites (46 BC and 25 BC) and Egypt in one (30 BC). Only Mauretania retained some independence and neither King Juba II, who ruled it at the date of this map, nor the Roman Emperor Augustus, who had put him on the throne, had any doubts that this independence had strict limits: for all practical purposes Mauretania was just another province and Juba a Roman proconsul.

Augustus made it his job to see that the Roman empire had sensible frontiers. In Europe he chose the Rhine and Danube as his boundaries, in the east the Euphrates, and in Africa the edge of the desert. In most instances he had a look at the possibilities of advancing further, but in Africa there was never really any case for doing so: two punitive expeditions – one to the oases of the Fezzan, one into Nubia as far as Napata – made it clear that there was nothing to be gained by pushing further south. The inhabitants were too few and too poor and communications too difficult. Just how right Augustus was is shown by the fact that the frontiers he drew lasted with only minor changes for more than 400 years.

Important though the establishment of Roman rule in North Africa obviously is, it is completely outclassed by a contemporary event that has a good claim to be *the* most important happening in African history – the outpouring of Negro tribes from West Africa across the centre of the continent. This spread two groups of Negroes, the Zande and the Bantu, along parallel tracks that extended from the Cameroon Mountains – the original eastern limit of the Negro peoples – through the northern part of the Zaire basin to the head waters of the White Nile. As Augustus put the finishing touches to the empire of Rome, the Zande and the Bantu opened up equatorial Africa: as Roman enterprise petered out in the wastes of the Sahara the Bantu reached the fertile lands of the western rift and the Lake Victoria region. Here they could multiply and gather strength for the next stage in their expansion.

The languages spoken by the Negro peoples at this time all belong to the same 'Niger–Congo' family. This has six divisions, of which two, Zande and Bantu, can be seen as products of the Iron Age migrations. The other four divisions – the West Atlantic group, Kwa, Mande and Voltaic – remained confined to West Africa; indeed at this stage it is safe to assume that each was still confined to the sector of West Africa where it had originally evolved. This means that as shown on the map, the west coast was exclusively occupied by people speaking languages of the West Atlantic family (Wolof and Fulani are the best known today), the southern coast by people speaking languages of the Kwa family (Kru, the Akan dialects and such southern-Nigerian languages as Yoruba and Igbo), the upper Senegal–upper Niger region by Mande speakers (Malinke, Soninke, Bambara) and the upper Volta by Voltaic-speaking tribes like the Mossi.

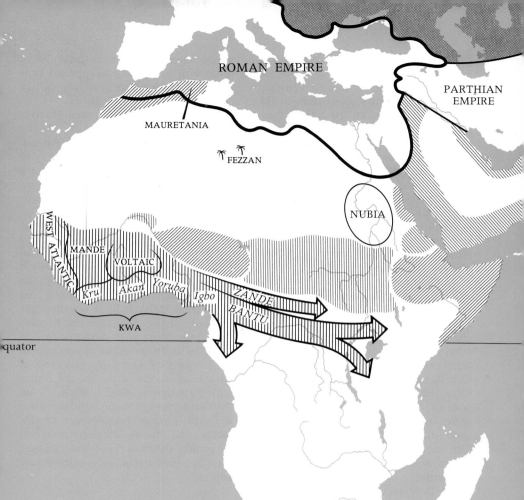

ROMAN EMPIRE

PARTHIAN
EMPIRE

MAURETANIA

FEZZAN

NUBIA

WEST ATLANTIC

MANDE

VOLTAIC

Kru   Akan Yoruba

Igbo

ZANDE

BANTU

KWA

Equator

AD 1

THIS map shows how the Bantu in the first two centuries AD exploited the favourable situation they had created for themselves in the last two centuries BC. First they completed their march across the continent by pushing forward from Lake Victoria to the Indian Ocean: this made it certain that one day all the lands to the south would belong to them. Then they began to occupy these lands by moving down the Zaire (this is hypothetical: we have no radiocarbon dates for the Atlantic side) and through East Africa (where the most rapid progress seems to have been made via the western rift).[1]

As the Bantu advanced the Pygmies and Bushmen retreated, the Pygmies into the depths of their forests, the Bushmen to the south. There was no chance of these Stone Age food gatherers successfully resisting the Bantu, they were too few and too primitive for that. The Bantu, with their corn and their cattle, their iron weapons and their warrior castes, were like the *conquistadors* in the New World, operating on a quite different level from the natives. The natives in the African case fared better, however. The Pygmies learnt to live with the Bantu who surged around them: they survived and today speak Bantu languages. The Bushmen were pushed off most of their range but kept the Kalahari, their peculiar language of clicks and their ethnic identity.

By reducing the kingdom of Mauretania to provincial status (AD 42) the Romans completed their North African empire. This wasn't a military worry to them and never required more than a small garrison – usually only two or three of the empire's thirty legions. However, it was vital economically. It was the only part of the empire to produce a reliable surplus of wheat and on this surplus the city of Rome had come to depend. Every spring a fleet left Egypt carrying enough wheat to fill the city's granaries for a twelvemonth, and if anything delayed it, it was to other parts of North Africa that the Romans looked to make up the deficiency.

In the Horn, note the appearance of the kingdom of Axum, the precursor of Abyssinia. Axum, a ceremonial centre with Egyptian-inspired obelisks, is on the northern edge of the highland zone: it is the further development of this sector that marks the emergence of Abyssinia; the coastal province, Eritrea, then becomes a relatively unimportant adjunct.

1. The Bantu get a distinctive shading of their own now to mark their emergence as one of Africa's major stocks.

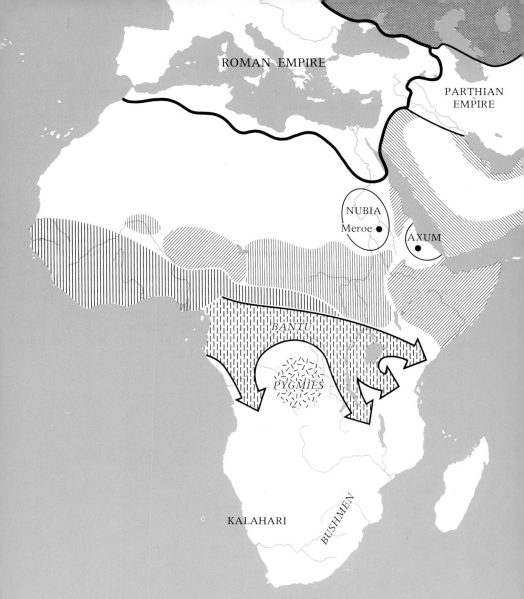

ROMAN EMPIRE

PARTHIAN
EMPIRE

NUBIA
Meroe

AXUM

BANTU

PYGMIES

KALAHARI

BUSHMEN

AD 200

THE population of the world in the Old Stone Age was very small, a matter of five million or so. Of this number Africa's share was about a million. In 5000 BC the introduction of agriculture started the continent's population graph on the upward course it has maintained ever since, though as farming remained restricted to Egypt for a long time the demographic development was at first curiously lopsided: between 5000 BC and 2000 BC the Egyptians multiplied up from 100,000 to two million, a twentyfold increase, while the rest of Africa's population only managed to double. At this point Egypt held half the continent's population.

In the last millennium BC the arrival of first the Phoenicians and then the Romans brought the rest of North Africa into the Mediterranean world: the population of the Maghreb now rose to respectable levels. By AD 200 there were as many people there as in Egypt – a balance that has been approximately maintained ever since – and the two between them contained about half the African total – a proportion that has been steadily eroded. For, though off to a late and sluggish start, Black Africa was now well stuck into its demographic development. The sustained numerical increase associated with the appearance of Iron Age societies had begun at both ends of the Sudan – in Nubia and, more importantly, in West Africa: the advance of the Bantu meant that the whole of the rest of sub-Saharan Africa was soon to be involved in the process. The Pygmies and Bushmen were the odd men out: their numbers remained low – around the 200,000 mark in each case – because their life style remained mesolithic.

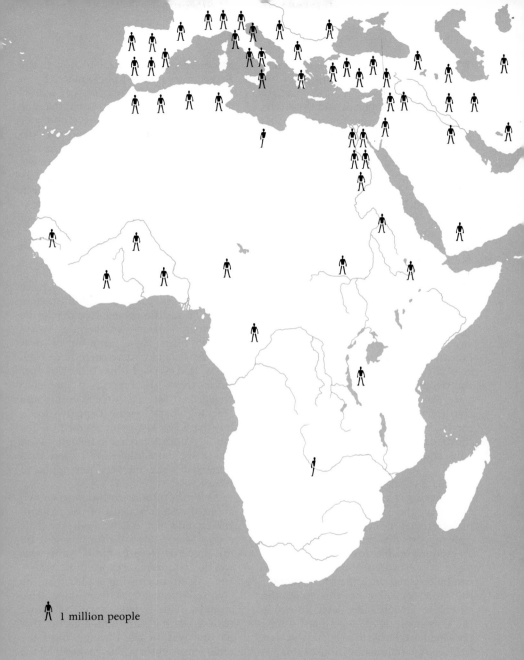

 1 million people

population in
AD **200**

W HAT the ancients knew of Africa's outline was discovered by two Asiatic peoples, the Phoenicians and the Arabs. By 2250 BC both were sailing regularly to Egypt, the Phoenicians with timber from the forests of the Lebanon, the Arabs with frankincense and myrrh from Arabia Felix, the present-day Yemen. There is no reason to believe that the Phoenicians at this time knew anything of Africa beyond the Nile delta: the Arabs on the other hand must have acquired a good working knowledge of both shores of the Red Sea and so mapped out, in their minds at least, a considerable stretch of Africa's coastline.

The Phoenicians of Tyre were responsible for the next advance, the exploration of the continent's Mediterranean coast. By their own account they started and finished this in the course of the twelfth century BC. No one questions the achievement, which is amply confirmed by the Tyrian monopoly of the trade with Spain in later centuries: the date is thought nowadays to be much later though, more like 800 BC than 1100.

Still, by 800 BC at the latest the Phoenicians were through the Pillars of Hercules (the strait of Gibraltar) and had founded Gades (Cadiz) in Spain. This suggests that they had reconnoitred an equivalent distance along the Atlantic coast of Morocco. Similarly the Arabs can be credited with the south shore of the Gulf of Aden by this time; this stretch of Somaliland – later known as the Cinnamon Coast – can hardly have remained unknown to seamen who were habitually circumnavigating Arabia.

How much further did the seamen of the classical world get? The answer, on the Atlantic side, is not far. The furthest certain point is the level of the Canaries, 'the Fortunate Islands'. These were discovered by fishermen from Cadiz in the first century BC and fully explored by an expedition sent by King Juba of Mauretania. They were uninhabited at the time (though it was only a short while later that a Stone Age Berber people, the Guanches, moved in from the mainland) and were not colonized: this, together with the fact that for centuries afterwards they were placed at the western end of the known world, strongly suggests that they marked the limit of classical voyaging.

On the east coast progress was much greater. The Cape of Perfumes (Cape Gardafui) was rounded, and twenty-three days' sail to the south, at a place called Rhapta, the Arabs established an entrepôt for the commodity that made this long journey worthwhile, ivory. Rhapta must have been on or near Zanzibar island, where there have been posts that served this function ever since: there are reports of one ship engaged in the trade overshooting and reaching a Cape Prasum (Cape Delgado ?) but that's the last point claimed. A line joining Capes Bojador and Delgado, as on this map, more likely overstates than understates the ancients' perception of Africa.

As for the interior nothing was known about the Sahara south of the oases of Fezzan and not much about the Nile above Meroe. Two centurions sent by the Emperor Nero to see if Nubia was worth conquering reported it wasn't, and, as an interesting aside, that the (White) Nile emerged from impassable swamps. This is true: they had either seen or heard of the Sudd, a barrier that no one was to get through until the nineteenth century. This makes it all the more remarkable that Ptolemy, who mapped the known world in the middle of the second century AD, was able to get the Nile above the Sudd so nearly right. He shows it rising in a mountain range in

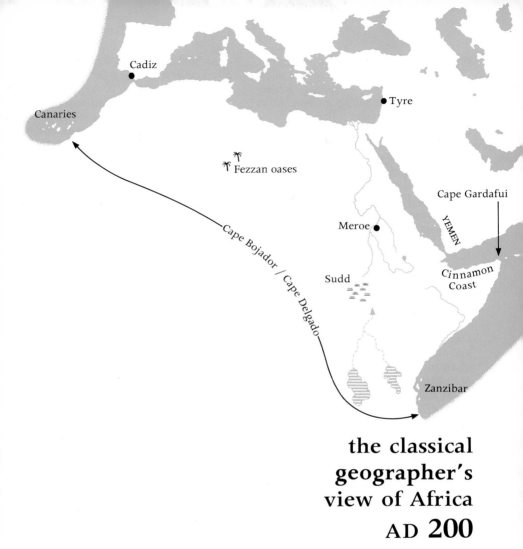

Cadiz

Tyre

Canaries

Fezzan oases

Cape Gardafui

Cape Bojador / Cape Delgado

Meroe

YEMEN

Sudd

Cinnamon
Coast

Zanzibar

the classical
geographer's
view of Africa
AD **200**

East Africa, the headstreams collecting into two large lakes before joining up and flowing north. Presumably this was a mixture of hearsay knowledge of Lakes Victoria and Albert acquired from the Arabs of Zanzibar and inspired speculation on the part of the geographer.

Left unanswered was the biggest question of all, was it possible to sail round Africa or not? Some said no, some said maybe and some said it had actually been done once, in the time of Pharaoh Necho (610–594 BC). The story was that Necho had sent some ships manned by Phoenicians off down the Red Sea and that they had reappeared three years later through the Pillars of Hercules. This is certainly no more than a tall tale: not many people believed it at the time and no one at all does today.

THINGS started to go wrong for the Roman empire in the third century AD: barbarian hordes poured across its European and Asian frontiers, the currency collapsed and for a few years it looked as if the whole structure was going to be swept away. Eventually the crisis was resolved but the empire that emerged from the ordeal was much altered: it was Christian, it was usually split into eastern and western halves, it was a bit smaller and it was a lot poorer.

In the early fifth century a second barbarian onslaught began. This time only the eastern half of the empire came through, the western half foundered. The capital of the west, Rome, was put to the sack first by the Goths (410) and then by the Vandals (455); the western provinces became the kingdoms of these and other German tribes. Or at least most of them did. In some, like Britain and Mauretania, power simply devolved on to the native chiefs. In North Africa this process had begun before the German invasions: it seems to have been part of a longer-term swing back from agriculture to pastoralism that had started as early as the third century.

As Rome's sun was setting Abyssinia emerged into the half light. The kings of Axum enlarged the area under their direct control, established some sort of suzerainty over the Arabs of the Yemen and, when provoked by the Nubians, hit back so hard that the kingdom of Meroe broke up into the three petty states shown on the map. The Axumites also adopted Christianity, the first royal house outside Rome's direct sphere of influence to do so.

Further to the south note the continuing expansion of the Bantu and the colonization of Madagascar. The nuclear Malagasy population amounted to a few boatloads of Indonesians who, if they had set out with the idea of colonizing somewhere, can hardly have known where they were going to end up: certainly they were never in contact with their homeland (Sumatra?) after they left it and probably never received any reinforcements, accidental or otherwise. This sort of blind voyaging sounds impossibly optimistic and obviously involves great risks. It is however perfectly sensible in biological terms and the Polynesians covered the whole Pacific in just this hit or miss way.

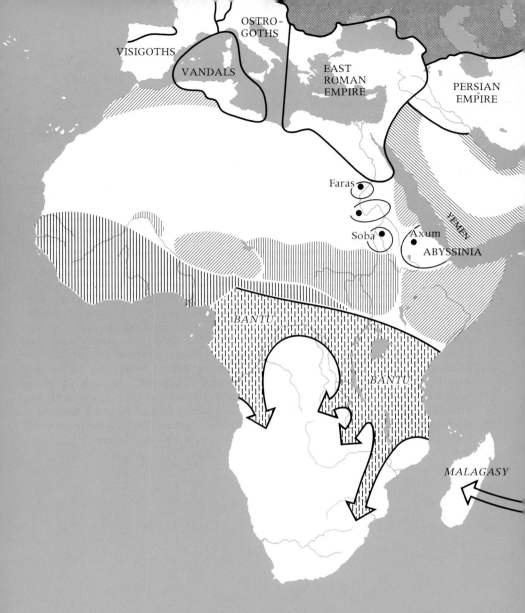

VISIGOTHS

OSTRO-
GOTHS

VANDALS

EAST
ROMAN
EMPIRE

PERSIAN
EMPIRE

Faras

YEMEN

Soba

Axum

ABYSSINIA

BANTU

BANTU

MALAGASY

AD **500**

THE sixth century was a good one for the eastern Roman empire: task forces sent out by the Emperor Justinian defeated the Vandals and Ostrogoths and brought Tunisia and Italy under imperial rule again; in the Mediterranean at least, Roman authority was almost completely restored. Roman missionaries didn't do so well: only the little Nubian principalities were added to the list of Christian states and beyond the Roman frontier Christians were still as likely as not to be persecuted for their faith.

One of the areas where Christians were particularly liable to massacre was Arabia. When this happened the survivors appealed to the Abyssinian king, the nearest Christian potentate, for protection and, if conditions in Abyssinia allowed it, he obliged with a punitive expedition. Normally these expeditions didn't go beyond the Yemen, but in 570 an Abyssinian army was despatched against the pagans of Mecca in the Hejaz. With it went an elephant, something never seen in these parts before. There was a great deal of excitement about this and though the expedition never actually got to Mecca – some sort of epidemic broke out and it turned back well short of the city – the elephant found a permanent place in local folklore. For it was in Mecca in 'the year of the elephant' that the Prophet Mohamed was born.

Mohamed, like most religious reformers, was rejected by his own people: success came only when he left Mecca and moved to Medina (622). Once there he soon became a power in the land and by the time he died ten years later most of the Arabian peninsula acknowledged his leadership. His successors, the Caliphs, were able to use the devotion he had inspired, the discipline he had imposed and the armies he had created to astonish the world. In a series of lightning campaigns these unknown warriors from the desert completely destroyed the Persian state and nearly wrecked the eastern Roman empire. In Africa they seized Egypt (640–42) and Cyrenaica and Tripolitania (642–7). By 650 they had established Mohamed's doctrine of Islam – 'submission (to Allah)' – as one of the world's great religions.

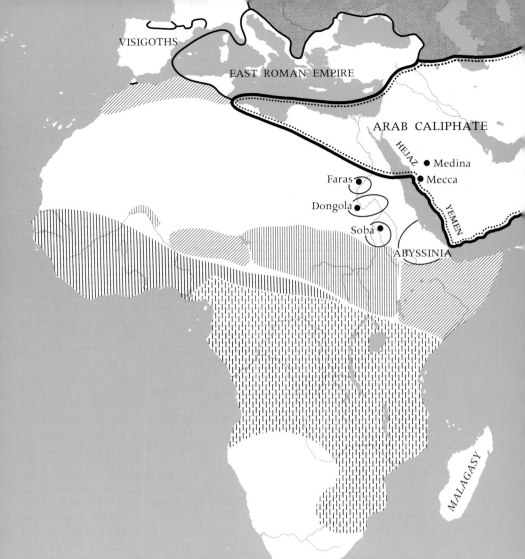

VISIGOTHS

EAST ROMAN EMPIRE

ARAB CALIPHATE

HEJAZ

● Medina

Faras

Mecca

Dongola

YEMEN

Soba

ABYSSINIA

MALAGASY

AD 650

THE Arabs' first attempt to conquer the Maghreb was made in 670–83: after some spectacular successes it ended in equally spectacular failure. In 694 they tried again. This time their progress was steady and complete. The Byzantines (east Romans) were expelled from the coastal cities, the Berber tribes of the interior subdued one by one. By 705 the Maghreb was finally incorporated in the Islamic world.

From the Maghreb al-Aqsa – the 'far west' meaning present-day Morocco – the Arab victors turned north against Spain and south against the Sanhaja Berbers. The kingdom of Spain succumbed immediately (711): the Sanhaja only gradually and in an ill-recorded and undramatic way. Nevertheless the advance to the south was of at least as much significance to Islam as its dominion in Spain. The Sanhaja had recently discovered how to live in the Sahara and how to cross it. They had found the way to Bilad as-Sudan, 'the land of the blacks'.

The Sanhaja started their trans-Saharan journeys from the Wadi Draa: in the central Sahara they took rock salt from deposits they had discovered in the course of their explorations, and on the banks of the Senegal they exchanged this salt for gold dust on a pound-for-pound basis. Even allowing for the high cost of travel in the desert, this was good business.

The Sanhaja were able to get to Senegal because of their skill as camel drivers. The camel is not native to Africa, it is an Asiatic animal first introduced by the Persians (to Egypt in the sixth century BC), first heard of in the Maghreb in Julius Caesar's time (first century BC) and not common there before the late Roman period (fourth century AD). There seems to have been some difficulty in establishing breeding herds but even so the realization of the camel's potential was extraordinarily slow: the Sanhaja were clearly the first people to make full use of the 'ship of the desert'.

It was Berber merchants visiting the Sahel who brought back reports of the first Negro state we know of, the Soninke kingdom of Ghana. This lay to the north of the gold-producing area (which at this time was the Bambuk field south of the upper Senegal) but managed to establish such a complete monopoly of gold sales that to the Arab world Ghana itself was the land of gold.

On the other side of Africa, on the Red Sea, the Abyssinians foolishly provoked the Arabs by various acts of piracy including, in 702, the sack of Jeddah, the port of Mecca. The Arabs retaliated by occupying the Eritrean coastline, forcing the Abyssinians back into their highlands. The Christians in this part of the world, Abyssinians and Nubians both, were now entirely cut off from their co-religionists in Europe and Asia Minor: with the absorption of Faras by Dongola in the early eighth century the number of Christian kingdoms in the continent fell from four to three.

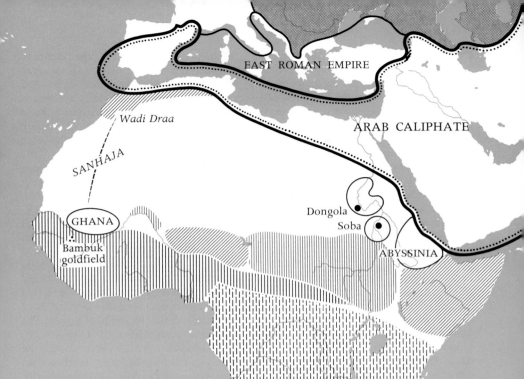

EAST ROMAN EMPIRE

ARAB CALIPHATE

Wadi Draa

SANHAJA

GHANA

Bambuk
goldfield

Dongola

Soba

ABYSSINIA

AD **750**

THE Sanhaja did not have a monopoly of the trans-Saharan trade for long. Within fifty years of the first contacts between the Maghreb and the western Sudan two more trans-Saharan routes were in regular operation: one from western Algeria to the middle Niger, one from Tripolitania to Lake Chad. These routes passed through the territory of the Tuareg, an offshoot of the Sanhaja who had colonized the central section of the Sahara: they opened up the way to Sudanese countries whose names now make their first appearance in contemporary accounts — the kingdom of Kanem on the east side of Lake Chad, the kingdom of the Songhay on the middle Niger and, beyond Ghana in the west, the kingdom of Mali.

Most of the chronicles of later times describe the founding dynasties of these kingdoms as white, meaning Berber or Arab. Perhaps they really were; much more likely they weren't and the founding legends were made up later to give the royal house a respectable ancestry in Mohamedan eyes. That the common people (and for that matter all the later kings) were entirely black is beyond doubt. In Ghana and Mali this means Negroes of the Mande group (Soninke in Ghana and Malinke (Mandingo) in Mali): in Kanem it means the Kanuri who were Nilo-Saharans like the Songhay.

Islam by this time had long since ceased to be run from Arabia, in fact it had almost ceased to be run at all. Though most of the Islamic world acknowledged the spiritual supremacy of the caliphs of Bagdad, the provincial governors of what had once been a united Arab empire had now made themselves into independent hereditary rulers. In North Africa there were two dynasties of this sort, the Aghlabids of Tunisia and the Tulunids of Egypt. The two other dynasties of the Islamic west, the Idrisids of Morocco and the Umayyads of Spain, went further than this; they didn't recognize the authority of Bagdad in any way at all.

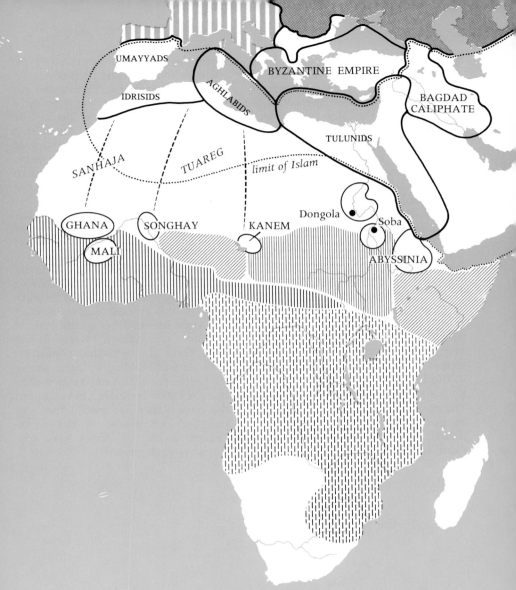

UMAYYADS

IDRISIDS

AGHLABIDS

BYZANTINE EMPIRE

BAGDAD
CALIPHATE

TULUNIDS

SANHAJA

TUAREG

limit of Islam

GHANA

SONGHAY

KANEM

Dongola •

Soba •

MALI

ABYSSINIA

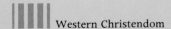 Western Christendom

AD **900**

EVEN in the palmiest days of the caliphs of Bagdad some Moslems had refused to regard them as anything but usurpers: according to these dissidents the caliphate belonged to the descendants of Fatima, the prophet's daughter, and to them alone. By the tenth century secret societies working in favour of Fatimid candidates existed throughout the Moslem world. Their members, who called themselves Shi'a Moslems (Moslems of the (secret) party), made skilful use of local discontents to promote their cause.

In 902 a Shi'a-inspired revolt broke out in eastern Algeria. It had such success that its leader was able to send off to Syria for the head of the Fatimid line, known to the Shi'a faithful as the Mahdi, the Saviour. By 912 the Mahdi was ruling Tunisia and Algeria from a newly founded capital city named – as seemed only right – Mahdiya.

The line of Fatimid caliphs founded by the Mahdi went on to great things. The most important was the conquest of Egypt in 969. There the Fatimids built themselves a second capital, the city of Cairo, to which they soon moved permanently. From Cairo they ruled Egypt, Palestine and the nearer parts of Arabia. They left Tripolitania, Tunisia and Algeria to a semi-independent dynasty of governors known as the Zirids. The Zirids, who were a Sanhaja family that had provided the Fatimids with support at a critical moment in their history, even managed to conquer Morocco briefly, so completing Fatimid control of North Africa.

One bit of political juggling that the Fatimids carried out soon after their move to Cairo was to have important consequences later. They arranged for the transfer of two Arab tribes, the Benu Hilal and the Benu Sulaym, from Arabia to Upper Egypt. According to the Fatimids this was a punishment inflicted on the Arabs for rebelling against Fatimid rule, but one wonders if it was really like that. There are signs that population pressure was building up again among the bedouin of Arabia and it may well be that the Fatimids couldn't have stopped the move if they had tried. Either way the Arab component in the northeastern corner of Africa was considerably strengthened.

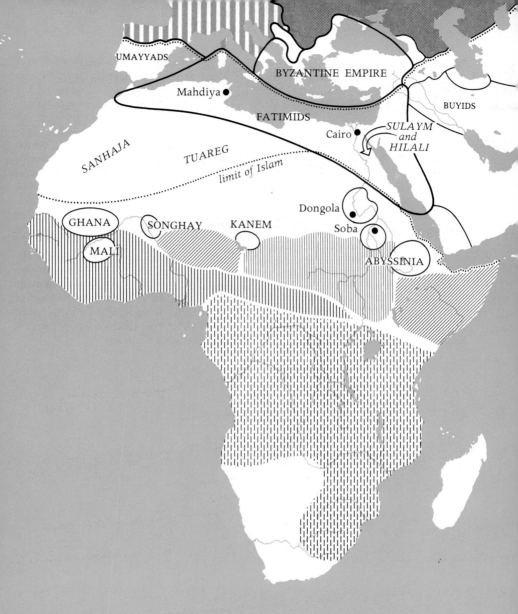

UMAYYADS

BYZANTINE EMPIRE

Mahdiya

FATIMIDS

BUYIDS

Cairo

SULAYM and HILALI

SANHAJA

TUAREG

limit of Islam

GHANA

SONGHAY

KANEM

Dongola

Soba

MALI

ABYSSINIA

‖‖‖‖ Western Christendom

AD **975**.

WITHIN seventy-five years of the move to Cairo the Fatimid empire in North Africa was reduced to Egypt. First Morocco broke away (980), then the Zirid principalities of eastern Algeria (1014) and Tunisia–Tripolitania (1049). The Fatimids got their revenge on the Zirids by encouraging the Benu Hilal and Benu Sulaym to attack them: these two bedouin tribes, which were already on the move west from Egypt, were only too happy to oblige. Over the next few years the Benu Sulaym occupied Cyrenaica and Tripolitania, while the Benu Hilal defeated the main Zirid army and overran the interior of Tunisia.

The nomads of the western Sahara, the Sanhaja Berbers, were also on the offensive. Their inspiration was provided by a puritanical Moslem sect with its headquarters at a secret *ribat* – a monastery run on military lines – which was probably situated on one of the Tidra Islands off the Mauritanian coast: its members called themselves *al-murabitun*, the men of the monastery, hence Almoravids, the name by which they are known to Western historians. Almoravid preaching was so successful that by the early 1050s most of the Sanhaja had been won over to the sect. The new power quickly showed its strength – and range – by seizing the towns at either end of the western trans-Saharan trade route, Sijilmasa in the north (1054) and Awdaghost in the south (1055). The Almoravids also made an alliance with the Tokolor Negroes of the middle Senegal who had converted to Islam a generation earlier – the first Negro people to do so.

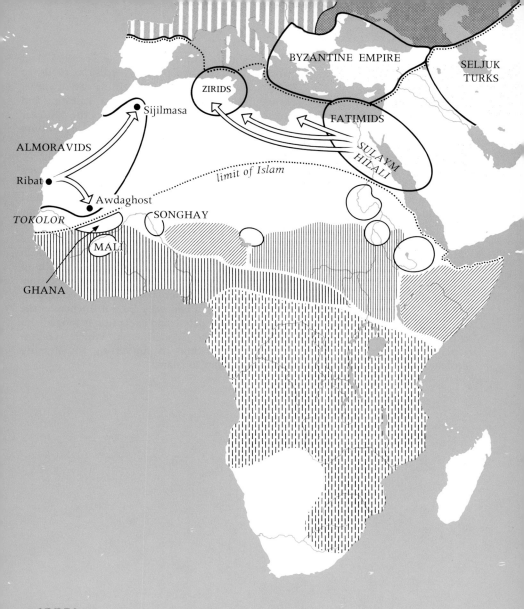

BYZANTINE EMPIRE

SELJUK
TURKS

ZIRIDS

FATIMIDS

Sijilmasa

ALMORAVIDS

SULAYM
HILALI

Ribat

limit of Islam

Awdaghost

TOKOLOR

SONGHAY

MALI

GHANA

Western Christendom

AD **1055**

THE nomads had done well throughout the Moslem world during the 1050s: in the remaining decades of the eleventh century they did even better. In the far west, Almoravid armies overwhelmed the countries north and south of their part of the Sahara, conquering Morocco and western Algeria between 1056 and 1082, and Ghana and the Songhay between 1076 and 1083; Moslem Spain was eventually added to this Almoravid empire, most of it before 1100. In eastern Algeria and Tunisia the successful nomad power was that of the Hilalian Arabs: outside a few coastal cities – notably Bougie and Mahdiya, where Zirid princes were still holding out – their domination of this area in 1100 was virtually complete. So was that of the Sulaym in Cyrenaica and Tripolitania. However, the really spectacular nomad achievement was in the Moslem east. There the Seljuk Turks rode out from Iran, where they had established themselves in the 1050s, to take just about everything east of Suez – Iraq, the Caucasus, Syria, Palestine and the Hejaz. They also broke the 400-year stalemate between Islam and Byzantium by inflicting an annihilating defeat on the Byzantine army at Manzikert (1071). Though the Christian counterattack known as the First Crusade did well in Syria and Palestine it achieved almost nothing in Anatolia. The Turk had come to Turkey to stay.

In the course of the tenth century the Arabs who traded along the East African coast started to build up a chain of settlements there. Where possible they chose offshore islands for these outposts, so they had very little influence on the local people: an exception is Mogadishu on the Somali coast, which was instrumental in converting the near-by tribes to Islam.

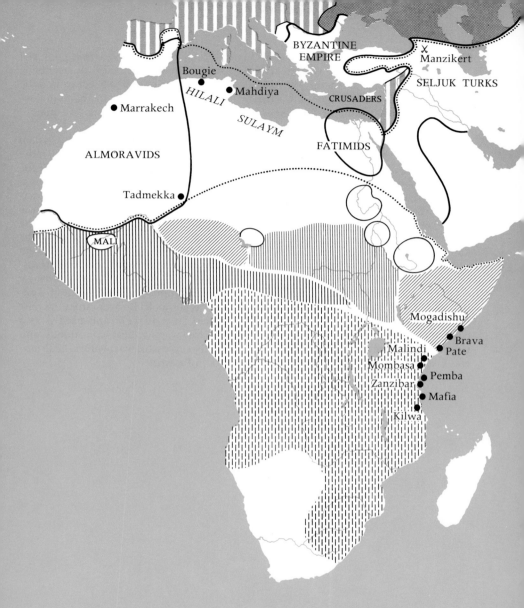

BYZANTINE
EMPIRE

Manzikert

SELJUK TURKS

Bougie

HILALI

Mahdiya

CRUSADERS

Marrakech

SULAYM

FATIMIDS

ALMORAVIDS

Tadmekka

MALI

Mogadishu

Brava
Pate

Malindi
Mombasa

Pemba

Zanzibar

Mafia

Kilwa

AD **1100**

THE empire of the Almoravids collapsed in the mid twelfth century. In the north, in Morocco and Spain, they were replaced by the Almohads, a rather similar religious sect – the name, strictly spelt *al-muwayidun*, means 'those who proclaim the unity of God' – which represented the political as well as the religious aspirations of the Sanhaja's arch enemies, the Zenata Berbers of the Atlas. In the south, in Ghana, the Almoravids were ejected as part of a Negro and animist reaction that put a new Soninke dynasty, the Susu of Kaniaga, in power.

The revived Ghana of the Susu did not extend quite so far west as its predecessor – the Soninke of Diafunu remained outside its control – but it did conquer Mali to the south and so gained control of the Bure goldfield. This was important because production from Bure was fast overtaking the output from the traditional source of Sudanese gold, the Bambuk field. The shift in economic interest from Senegal to Niger caused the west Saharan caravans to abandon Awdaghost in favour of Walata, 240 miles to the east.

Apart from the setback in Mali, Islam was doing well. In the central Sudan the Saifawa kings of Kanem adopted the faith, in the eastern sector of the Abyssinian highlands the Moslem principality of Shoa emerged as a rival to the Christian monarchy that still held the western sector, and in the Horn the Somali tribes were now as often Moslem as not. Moreover, Egypt had been transformed into a major military power by Saladin, founder of the Ayyubid dynasty, who took it over from its last Fatimid ruler in 1171 and used it as a base for waging near continuous and usually successful war against the Crusaders in Palestine.

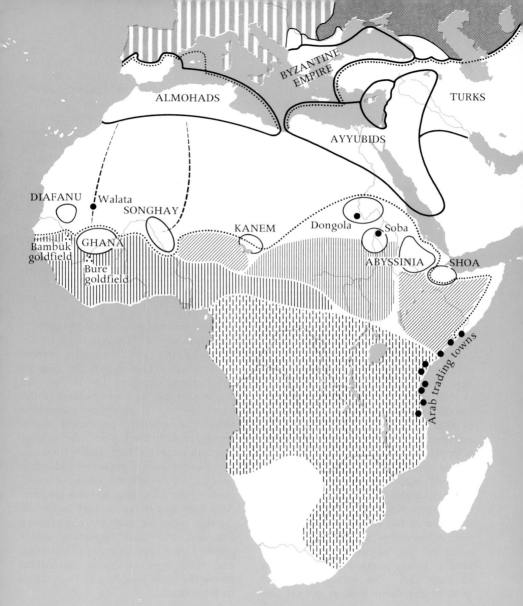

BYZANTINE
EMPIRE

ALMOHADS

TURKS

AYYUBIDS

DIAFANU • Walata

SONGHAY

KANEM

Dongola •

Soba •

GHANA

Bambuk
goldfield

Bure
goldfield

ABYSSINIA

SHOA

Arab trading towns

AD 1200

COVERING as it did the straightforward west-to-east unit formed by Morocco, Algeria and Tunisia, the Almohad empire looked a better political proposition than the north-and-south, either-side-of-the-Sahara empire of the Almoravids. Actually it fell apart just as quickly. During the 1230s the governors of Tunisia and Algeria established their independence: the success of the dynasties they founded – Hafsid in Tunisia (from 1236) and Ziyanid in Algeria (from 1239) – demonstrated that the natural state of the Maghreb was the tripartite division we have today. The Almohads kept control of their Moroccan homeland for another thirty years: then, in 1269, they lost that too, being replaced by the nominees of another Zenata clan, the Banu Marin.

South of the Sahara the thirteenth century was notable for the rise to empire of two Negro states, one old, one new. The one we have already met with is Mali which, at the beginning of this period, was subjected to the Susu kings of Ghana. In the 1230s Mali's independence was re-established by a Malinke prince named Sundiata: by the end of his reign Sundiata was master not only of Mali but of Ghana, Walata, Tadmekka and the Songhay. This was the biggest empire the western Sudan had seen so far. It was also the wealthiest. When one of Sundiata's successors went on the pilgrimage to Mecca – which, being pious Moslems, several of them did – he brought so much gold to the Cairo bullion market that the price of the metal fell 20 per cent.

The other Negro empire appeared about as far away from Mali as possible – in Rhodesia, 3,500 miles to the southeast. It was also heavily involved in the gold trade, in this case as a primary producer. Small deposits of gold-bearing ores occur on the surface on the Rhodesian plateau and in the course of the thirteenth century the Bantu people who lived there, the Shona, began to exploit these in an organized way. The gold was marketed at Sofala, an outpost the Arabs of Kilwa established specifically for this trade: the profits supported the impressive court of the Shona monarch at Great Zimbabwe, and made Kilwa the most prosperous of all the towns on the east coast.

Elsewhere the main point to notice is the displacement of the Ayyubids by the Mamluks in Egypt. Mamluk means slave, which at first sight might seem an unpromising thing to be: in fact the Egyptian army, like many others in the Islamic world at this time, consisted largely of specially purchased slaves (mostly young Turks) and the title of Mamluk was an honourable one. In Egypt the seizure of power by a Mamluk general in 1250 was marked by a resurgence of the crusading zeal that the later Ayyubids had conspicuously lacked. A regular series of military expeditions followed: the most important extinguished the Christian states of Palestine and Syria; a minor one within Africa shook the little kingdom of Dongola to its foundations.

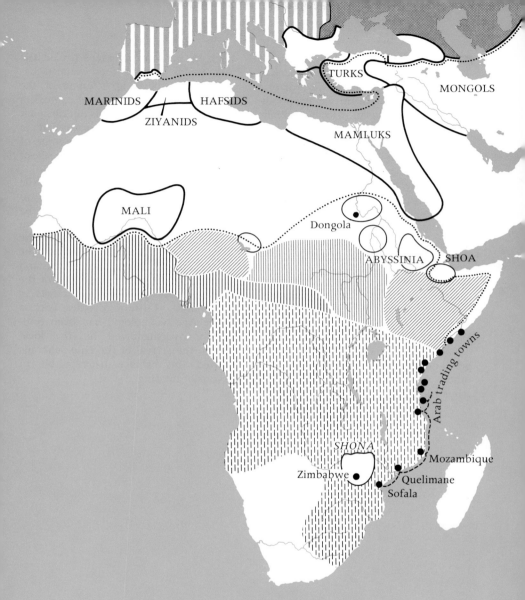

MARINIDS

HAFSIDS

ZIYANIDS

TURKS

MONGOLS

MAMLUKS

MALI

Dongola

ABYSSINIA

SHOA

Arab trading towns

SHONA

Zimbabwe

Mozambique

Quelimane

Sofala

AD **1300**

THE kingdom of Dongola didn't long survive the Mamluk sack of its capital in 1276: we hear of a puppet king – a Moslem – being appointed by the Mamluks in 1315, but both he and the royal authority disappeared for good when the Juhayna Arabs swept in from the north-east a few years later. Since the exodus of the Hilali and Sulaym in the eleventh century the bedouin of Upper Egypt's eastern desert had been relatively quiet: now either multiplication or reinforcement from Arabia had brought them to migration point again. The Juhayna mostly settled along the Nubian segment of the Nile – the stretch between the second and sixth cataracts. Some of them went further, however, taking their flocks across the western desert to the scanty pastures of Darfur and Kordofan.

South of the sixth cataract Soba lingered on for a while yet: east of Soba the other surviving Christian kingdom, Abyssinia, staged a remarkable come-back. A new line of kings (called the Solomonids because they claimed descent from the King Solomon of the Bible) not only checked the Moslem advance into the highlands but turned it right back. Then they proceeded to conquer the pagan tribes living south of the Blue Nile, nearly doubling the size of their kingdom by doing so (1316–30).

The situation along the White Nile was also changing at this time. Two groups of Nilo-Saharan pastoralists, the Madai and the Kalenjin, moved down from the area immediately south of the Sudd to the north-western shore of Lake Victoria (in the case of the Madai) and the Kenya highlands (in the case of the Kalenjin). The previous pastoralists in these areas, Cushitic peoples with a Stone Age technology, had been completely overshadowed by the local Bantu: the arrival of the Nilo-Saharans shifted the balance back a bit in favour of herding.

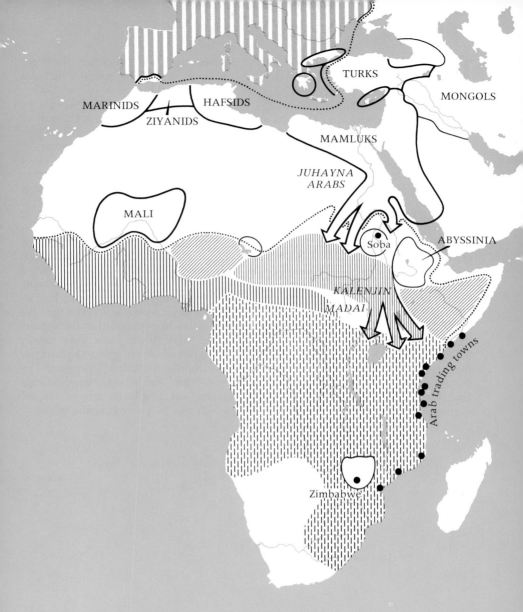

MARINIDS
ZIYANIDS
HAFSIDS
TURKS
MONGOLS
MAMLUKS
JUHAYNA ARABS
MALI
Soba
ABYSSINIA
KALENJIN MADAI
Arab trading towns
Zimbabwe

AD **1350**

KNOWLEDGE of Africa's outline was little greater in AD 1350 than in AD 200. On the west Cape Bojador still marked the limit of voyaging by ship; on the east the extension of the traditional trade route past Cape Delgado to Sofala brought with it the discovery of the Comoro Islands – previously uninhabited but soon to be settled by a mixture of Arabs, Malagasy and Bantu – and of Madagascar. But even this small addition to knowledge wasn't really followed up. The Arabs used the same term – *al-Qmr* – to cover the Comoros and Madagascar: this suggests that they can hardly have seen much of Madagascar and certainly hadn't circumnavigated it.

Where the continent's geography had been clarified was in the western Sudan. The whole strip of the Sahel from the Senegal to Lake Chad was now a part of the Islamic world, regularly visited by the trans-Saharan caravans and therefore reasonably well documented in the centres of Islamic learning. Most was known about the lands where the Niger makes its arc to the north – the area covered by the empire of the Mali – relatively little about the Senegal or Lake Chad. And of course nothing at all about the lower course of the Niger. This was to have peculiar consequences.

Arab geographers kept Ptolemy's idea of a Nile rising in a mountain range in East Africa and flowing north via a large lake. However, most of them also came to believe that the Niger was a branch of the Nile. Their idea was that the Niger – the 'Nile of the Negroes' as they called it – flowed via Lake Chad to Nubia: there it met the East African Nile and united with it to form the northward-flowing 'Nile of the Egyptians'. It was a bit far-fetched but at least it was better than the alternative hypothesis, that the reports of the Niger flowing east were simply wrong (which was to ignore the facts); or the additional flourish favoured by some, that the whole Niger–Senegal system was simply an arm of the sea (which was to ignore common sense).

Canaries

Cape Bojador

Niger

? *Lake Chad*

?

Sudd

Senegal | Sofala

Cape Delgado ━ Comoro Isles

Madagascar

**the medieval
geographer's
view of Africa
AD 1350**

THE medieval world didn't produce any explorers but it did have some great travellers. Undoubtedly the greatest was an African, Ibn Battuta. He was born in Tangier in 1304. In 1325 he set out on the pilgrimage to Mecca and having got there found he couldn't stop. Using Mecca as a base he visited all the countries of the Near East: he also made a voyage down the east coast of Africa to Mogadishu, Mombasa and Kilwa (1331). Then he moved to India, where he had some really extraordinary adventures.

Ibn Battuta came home to Morocco in 1349. Most of his journeying was done, but he still had two trips to do if he was to make good his claim to have visited every country in the Islamic world. One was easy: just a matter of crossing the Strait of Gibraltar and touring the little that was left of Moslem Spain. He did this the next year. The other took a lot more time and trouble. He began at Sijilmasa, where the trans-Saharan caravans formed up: his destination was the Sudan in general and Mali in particular.

Like most travellers Ibn Battuta was a bit of a liar, and he certainly never visited some of the places he said he had – China for instance. But no one has ever doubted his account of Mali: it's too detailed for that and his description of the strange mixture of Moslem and animist customs at the court of the king is entirely convincing. So are his rather priggish reactions, which range from admiration (for the high standards of security and justice) to scorn (for local ceremonial, especially in the matter of gifts for travelling scholars) and outrage (about the way the young girls dressed or, to be more accurate, didn't). One sombre note is the way the subject of slavery keeps coming up: when he set off home it was as part of a caravan taking 600 female slaves from Takedda to the north. It looks as though slaves were beginning to rival gold as the Sudan's most important export. There are hints of the same thing in his account of the east coast.

After his return to Morocco in 1353 Ibn Battuta finally settled down. The sultan provided him with a secretary and he dictated his memoirs to him. At the end of the final chapter the admiring scribe added a note of his own: 'It is plain to see', he said, 'that this shaykh is the traveller of the age.' And so it is.

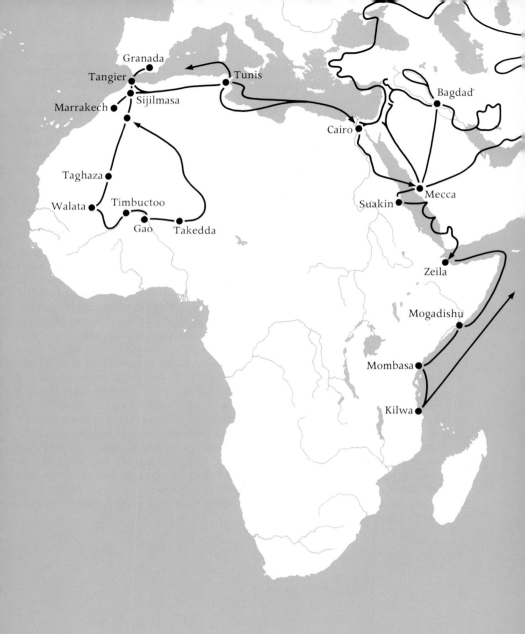

the travels of Ibn Battuta
AD **1325–53**

B Y 1400 the empire of Mali was past its best: it had lost control of the Songhay kingdom and the vague suzerainty it had once held over Senegal had vanished: the various sedentary peoples there recognized the paramountcy of the strongest local tribe, the Wolof, while the pastoralists, the Fulani, who were now beginning to expand eastward towards the Niger, recognized no one. Mali's most important asset, its control of the gold trade, it did retain for a little while longer and this despite a significant shift in the pattern of supply. New fields on the Black Volta and in the Akan Forest started producing for export at this time: their output was channelled north via Jenne to Timbuctoo, which consequently became an important departure point for trans-Saharan caravans.

With the fifteenth century we get our first historical information on the stretch of the Sahel between the Niger and Lake Chad. In the western and central parts of this area the Hausa city states – traditionally seven in number – were beginning to differentiate: Kano, Katsina, Zaria and Gobir being the important ones to start with. In the eastern sector the emerging political unit was the kingdom of Bornu, founded by a refugee king from Kanem who had been expelled from his own country by the Bulala. It is uncertain whether the Bulala were a clan or a tribe, a branch of the Kanuri people of Kanem or an invading hoard of pastoralists from the east: either way, by 1400, the throne of Kanem was in the hands of the Bulala, the royal house of Kanem had become kings in Bornu, and the original inhabitants of Bornu, the So (a Chadic people like the Hausa), were in danger of losing their ethnic and political identity.

Islam was now established among all the peoples of the Sahel from the Fulani of Senegal in the west to the Arabs of the upper Nile in the east. Its success was somewhat less than this implies, however, for Islam as practised in the Sahel would have raised plenty of eyebrows in Arabia: animist rituals continued side by side with Moslem observances in much the same way as Voodoo and Christian ceremonials overlap in present-day Brazil. This means that the line of dots showing the perimeter of the Islamic world shouldn't be taken too literally in its Sahel sector: it represents a band of territory within which Moslem influences fade out rather than a boundary between Moslem and non-Moslem communities. Anyhow, this is the last time the line will appear for a while; the advance of Islam is slowing down and there's no need to show the situation more than once every hundred years.[1]

1. When it does appear again, as on the political map for 1600, it is used to show Islam's southern boundary only, because the northern one is adequately defined by the banded tint marking the extent of Christendom. This marking, which from now on includes eastern as well as western Christianity, subsequently becomes the hallmark of the European colonialist advance into Africa.

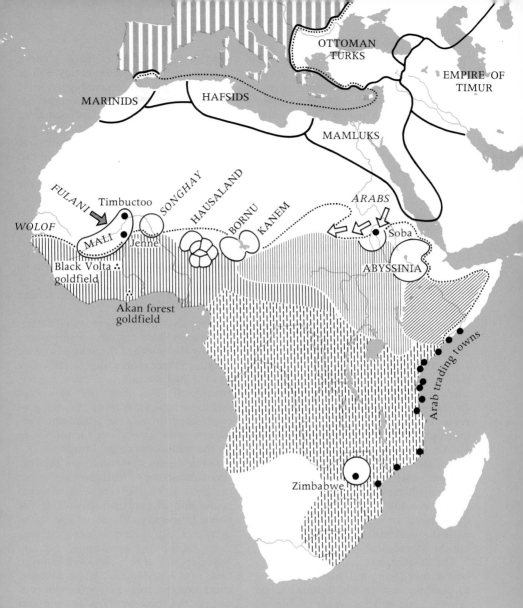

MARINIDS

HAFSIDS

OTTOMAN
TURKS

EMPIRE OF
TIMUR

MAMLUKS

FULANI

Timbuctoo

SONGHAY

HAUSALAND

BORNU

KANEM

ARABS

Soba

WOLOF

MALI

Jenne

ABYSSINIA

Black Volta
goldfield

Akan forest
goldfield

Arab trading towns

Zimbabwe

AD **1400**

IN the fifteenth century improved designs of ships appeared in Europe and China. The Chinese developed big (up to 2,000 ton), multi-masted vessels capable of sailing to the Indian Ocean and across it. Though they weren't discovering anything new in doing this – the Indian Ocean routes had been used by the Arabs for centuries – the distances they covered were impressive. In 1417 a Chinese fleet even visited East Africa. It collected some curiosities (including a giraffe) but the little trading it did can't conceivably have covered its expenses. And, curiosity satisfied, the Chinese never came back.

The Portuguese also launched a new design of ship, the caravel. It was much smaller than the Chinese ocean-going junks – usually displacing no more than 200 tons – but it was just as seaworthy and a lot cheaper to run. With it Prince Henry of Portugal was confident he could make voyages of exploration pay. He was particularly interested in Africa. As a young man of twenty-two he had taken part in Portugal's first successful overseas venture, the seizure of Ceuta (1415): from his interrogation of Moorish prisoners there he had learnt a lot about the trans-Saharan traffic in gold and slaves. Wouldn't it be easy to sail along the Atlantic coast, make direct contact with the merchants of Mali and so cut out the Moroccans?

The answer was no. Eighteen years later Prince Henry still hadn't managed to persuade any of his captains to go beyond Cape Bojador. What frightened them was the way the wind there always blew from the north: it just didn't seem possible for a ship to make it back against a wind as steady as this. Prince Henry had also failed to establish control over the motley crew of European adventurers who in 1402–5 had conquered the nearer islands of the Canary archipelago: they became vassals of Spain, not Portugal. However, the Portuguese had learned how to sail the open sea: their discoveries of Madeira (1420) and the Azores (1431) clearly demonstrated that. And they were slowly mastering the techniques needed to sail into a headwind. By 1434 one of Prince Henry's captains was confident enough to try Cape Bojador: he stood out to sea till he was thirty leagues past the Cape and then turned in, tacked back past it, and home.

After that things went much faster. Within ten years Portuguese ships were visiting the mouth of the Senegal and by the time Prince Henry died in 1460 they had reached Sierra Leone. Most important of all, the enterprise was now making a handsome profit. From a post established on Arguin Island the Portuguese were able to cut themselves in on the trans-Saharan gold trade.

Other points to mention are the further contraction of Mali (now no longer in control of the Jenne–Timbuctoo route) and the northward shift of the Shona kingdom in Rhodesia. The Shona completely abandoned their original capital, Zimbabwe, apparently because gold deposits near it were worked out: their new kingdom, known as Mutapa, contained the areas that were still producing, but these were few and the gold trade in this area was now definitely past its best.

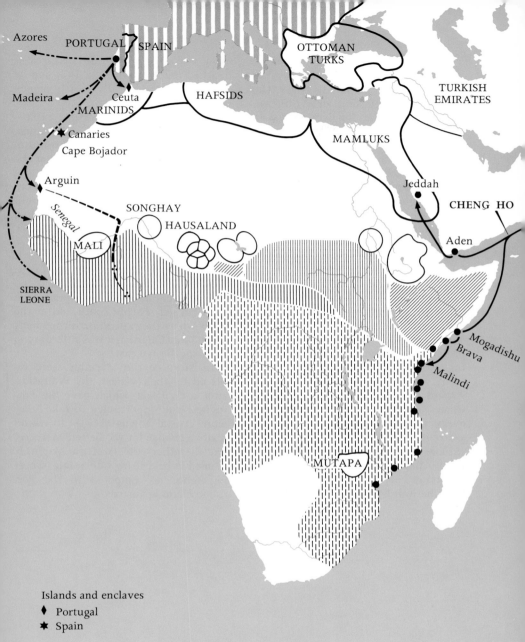

Azores

PORTUGAL SPAIN

Madeira

Ceuta
MARINIDS

Canaries
Cape Bojador

Arguin

HAFSIDS

OTTOMAN
TURKS

TURKISH
EMIRATES

MAMLUKS

Jeddah

CHENG HO

Aden

Senegal

SONGHAY

HAUSALAND

MALI

SIERRA
LEONE

Mogadishu
Brava

Malindi

MUTAPA

Islands and enclaves
♦ Portugal
★ Spain

AD 1460

AFTER Mali it was the turn of the Songhay to become the imperial power of the middle Niger. The new empire was the creation of King Ali, who ascended the Songhay throne in 1464, conquered Timbuctoo five years later and Jenne four years after that. This should have given him complete control of the output of the Akan and Black Volta goldfields. It didn't, because the Portuguese had now found the way to the Akan coast and the gold produced in the southern fields was going to them. The Portuguese got the geography in a bit of a muddle – they thought they had found Ghana, West Africa's original 'land of gold'. However, as they spelt it Guinea it isn't too difficult to distinguish Guinea from Ghana – or at least it wasn't until recently.

The discovery of Guinea was a bit of private enterprise. In 1469 the Portuguese crown granted a five-year monopoly of the African trade beyond Arguin to a Lisbon merchant, Fenão Gomes: in return Gomes promised that every year he would (a) pay 500 crusados into the royal treasury and (b) explore another 100 leagues of Africa's coast – quite stiff terms considering that any trade beyond Arguin was entirely hypothetical. But Gomes didn't have to wait very long for his profit: his captains reached the Akan coast in 1471 and he must have been literally coining money after that.

Guinea made Gomes a fortune: exploration beyond produced no return. Nevertheless it was an exciting venture. All the early reports indicated that the shore line of the Gulf of Guinea ran steadily east: this meant that a few more years at a hundred leagues a year would bring the Portuguese to the Indian Ocean and the riches of the oriental spice trade. Unfortunately the last voyage under Gomes' contract showed that it wasn't going to be quite as easy as that: beyond the island of Fernando Po (named after one of Gomes' captains) the coast turned sharply south and at the point where the expedition turned back (Cape Santa Caterina) it was still running more south than east.

In Morocco the Marinids were replaced by their viziers, the Wattasids, after a civil war which gave the Portuguese the opportunity to take some more coastal towns (1471). It wasn't really a change for the better. Morocco, like the other powers of the Maghreb, seemed to be drifting into a state of near impotence as compared to the Portuguese and Spaniards.

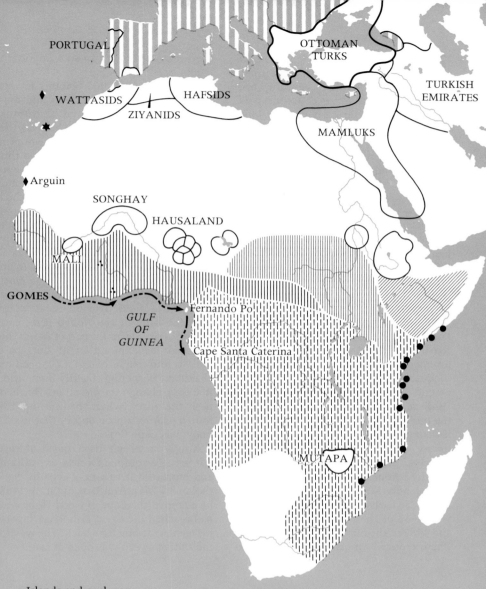

PORTUGAL

OTTOMAN
TURKS

TURKISH
EMIRATES

WATTASIDS

HAFSIDS

ZIYANIDS

MAMLUKS

Arguin

SONGHAY

HAUSALAND

MALI

GOMES

Fernando Po

*GULF
OF
GUINEA*

Cape Santa Caterina

MUTAPA

Islands and enclaves
◆ Portuguese
★ Spanish

AD **1475**

IN 1481 the fleet that left Lisbon for Guinea was much larger than usual. Portugal's African venture had rather hung fire since the ending of Gomes' contract: now a new king, John II, had decided to get things moving again. Aboard the ships were stonemasons, carpenters and a company of soldiers: their orders were to build, provision and garrison a permanent fort on the Akan coast.

By the end of 1482 King John had his fort. Because he thought that the gold of Guinea was mined (whereas really it was panned from alluvial deposits) he called it São Jorge da Mina – St George of the Mine – a name that was soon shortened to Elmina. It was Europe's first foothold in black Africa.

Elmina was built to ensure that only Portuguese ships traded on the Akan coast: King John wasn't going to have foreigners reaping the benefit of Portuguese discoveries. He also intended to extend the range of these discoveries. While most of the fleet was committed to the building of Elmina, two ships under the command of Diogo Cão were sent off to see what lay beyond Cape Santa Caterina. Each carried in its hold a *padrão*, a stone cross with an inscription stating how King John II had ordered Diogo Cão to discover these lands 'in the year 6681 of the creation of the world and 1482 of the birth of our Lord Jesus'. These crosses were to be used to mark the expedition's most important landfalls.

Actually it was 1483 before Cão was past Cape Santa Caterina and midsummer before he had found something worth one of his crosses. This was the Zaire River. His second *padrão* he put up at the furthest point he reached on this voyage, Cape Santa Maria, 600 miles to the south. From there he hurried home to break the news that he had reached the end of Africa and found the way to the Indies.

How he got this idea is a mystery: perhaps it was simply a psychological reaction to the long months spent in an unknown world. His next voyage must have soon shown him how wrong he had been. After a side trip up the Zaire to visit the king of the Kongo (the most powerful people in this part of Africa) he resumed his exploration of the coast only to find that although it changed its character, becoming steadily more arid, it didn't change its direction. He died near the place where he put up his fourth *padrão*, a promontory that is still known as Cape Cross.

King John wasn't discouraged, at least not yet. He equipped a new expedition and entrusted it to a new captain, Bartholomew Dias. And Dias did it: in 1488 he rounded the Cape of Good Hope and had reached the Great Fish River before his men made him turn back. The way to the Indian Ocean was open at last.

Elmina

Diogo CÃO 1482–6   Cape Santa Caterina

✝ mouth of the Zaire

✝ Cape Santa Maria

✝ Monte Negro

✝ Cape Cross

Bartholomew DIAS 1487–8   ✝ Luderitz

Cape of Good Hope   ✝ Kwaaihoek

✝ padrão

Portuguese voyages
AD **1482–8**

THOUGH Dias had found the way round Africa it had turned out to be much longer than anyone had expected. Was his discovery worth following up? Could anyone operate profitably over distances like these? It took the news of Columbus's safe return from his first voyage across the Atlantic to decide the argument: if Spain could find a fortune beyond the ocean, so could Portugal.

The time lost wasn't all wasted: when the Portuguese Indies expedition did finally set out (in 1497) it was well-found and had a carefully worked-out navigational plan for getting to the Cape of Good Hope. This involved sailing two sides of a triangle so as to make the best possible use of the prevailing winds (north-easterly in the central Atlantic, westerly in the latitude of the Cape): it was probably thought up by Dias, who is known to have been in charge of the building and fitting out of the four-ship flotilla. Unfortunately, Dias was of humble birth and the command of an expedition as important as this had to go to an aristocrat. The man on whom the king's choice fell was one of his courtiers, Vasco da Gama.

It has to be admitted that da Gama, despite his blue blood, carried out Dias's plan well enough. He turned a bit too soon, making an unintended landfall a hundred miles north of the Cape, but his three-month voyage from the Cape Verde Islands to the Cape of Good Hope – much the longest anyone had ever made on the open sea – showed that this was the right way to go about the journey: it cut the time to the Cape by half.

After rounding the Cape, da Gama broke up his biggest ship and distributed its supplies between the other three. Then he sailed on. He missed the nearest Arab trading post, the one at Sofala, but found the next, Quelimane, and so linked up with the East African trading system. Most of the Arabs he parleyed with were understandably hostile, but the fact that he got on particularly badly at Mombasa endeared him to the king of neighbouring Malindi. The king agreed to provide a pilot who would take the Portuguese to India: da Gama paid Malindi the compliment of planting his last *padrão* there. Four weeks later the Portuguese ships were in India loading spices. It had taken them ten months to get there from Lisbon; another ten and they were back in Lisbon again.

When Vasco da Gama set out, Africa still had two Christian kingdoms, Soba and Abyssinia. By the time he got back it was down to one: Soba had fallen to the Abdallabite Arabs. The Abdallabites were a clan of the Juhayna and their advance was a continuation of the Juhayna expansion that had begun in the north-east in the fourteenth century: it was disputed by the Funj, animists from the Abyssinian borderlands who were moving down the Blue Nile at this time.

Also worth a mention is the Songhay King Mohamed's raid into Hausaland in the course of which he sacked three of the four biggest of the Hausa cities, Gobir, Katsina and Zaria, and extracted tribute from the biggest of all, Kano.

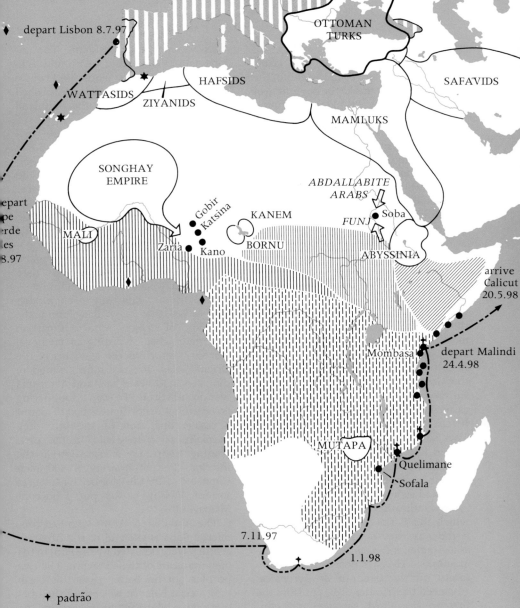

depart Lisbon 8.7.97

OTTOMAN
TURKS

WATTASIDS

HAFSIDS

ZIYANIDS

SAFAVIDS

MAMLUKS

depart
pe
rde
les
8.97

SONGHAY
EMPIRE

*ABDALLABITE
ARABS*

MALI

Gobir
Katsina

KANEM

FUNJ

Soba

Zaria
Kano

BORNU

ABYSSINIA

arrive
Calicut
20.5.98

Mombasa

depart Malindi
24.4.98

MUTAPA

Quelimane

Sofala

7.11.97

1.1.98

+ padrão
Islands and enclaves
♦ Portuguese
✴ Spanish

Vasco da Gama's
voyage to India
AD **1497–8**

IN the sense that the voyages of Columbus and Vasco da Gama opened up the world, the end of the fifteenth century marks the beginning of modern times. People's attitudes, though, remained medieval for a long time to come. Nowhere is this more noticeable than in the way religion continued to dominate politics: enmity between Christian and Moslem was assumed, warfare between the two continuous and the crusade and its Moslem equivalent, the *jihad*, remained part of everyone's political vocabulary.

Somewhat surprisingly the Christians didn't do at all well in this warfare during the sixteenth century: the Ottoman Turks were usually doing the attacking and usually winning. Though some of the Turkish advances were at the expense of other Moslem powers – most notably the overthrow and annexation of the empire of the Egyptian Mamluks by the Ottoman sultan Selim the Grim in 1516–17 – the Christians suffered egregious defeats. In southeastern Europe, Turkish arms swept all before them: in north-west Africa Turkish intervention turned what had looked like being an easily won Christian (specifically Spanish) hegemony over this anarchic area into a bitterly contested struggle.

One indication of the vigour with which the Turks conducted operations is the way they expanded the African and Arabian interests acquired from the Mamluks. They imposed their suzerainty on the bedouin of Cyrenaica, advanced the frontier of Egypt from the first to the third cataract and consolidated their position at the entrance to the Red Sea by garrisoning Zeila (1520) and Aden (1538). They also supplied a corps of musketeers to the sultan of Adal which enabled him to win a crushing victory over the Abyssinians. The unfortunate king of Abyssinia found himself hunted from one mountain fastness to another as the Moslems established themselves throughout the highland zone.

This was disappointing for the Portuguese. Their position in the Indian Ocean was entirely based on sea power, and though Portuguese admirals did brilliantly well with what resources they had – for example, they managed to keep the Arab cities of the East African coast in line without ever committing more than a handful of men ashore – they badly needed an ally on the mainland. In Christian Abyssinia they thought they had found a useful one – indeed for a while they even kidded themselves that they had found the kingdom of Prester John, a Christian potentate who, according to medieval rumour, terrorized the Moslems of the Orient. Alas, Prester John's kingdom didn't exist (it never had) and Abyssinia was no substitute. To stop it foundering completely the Portuguese had to mount a rescue operation of the sort they normally tried to avoid in the east, landing troops for a campaign in the interior. The little army – 400 men commanded by Christopher da Gama (a son of Vasco) – was put ashore at Massawa in 1541.

The Abdallabite Arabs who had conquered Soba at the end of the fifteenth century were defeated by the Funj in the opening years of the sixteenth. The two peoples got on better than this clash indicates: a balance was established between an Abdallabite viceroy ruling the northern half of the Funj kingdom, and the Funj monarch in the south. The subsequent conversion of the Funj to Islam helped cement this dyarchy.

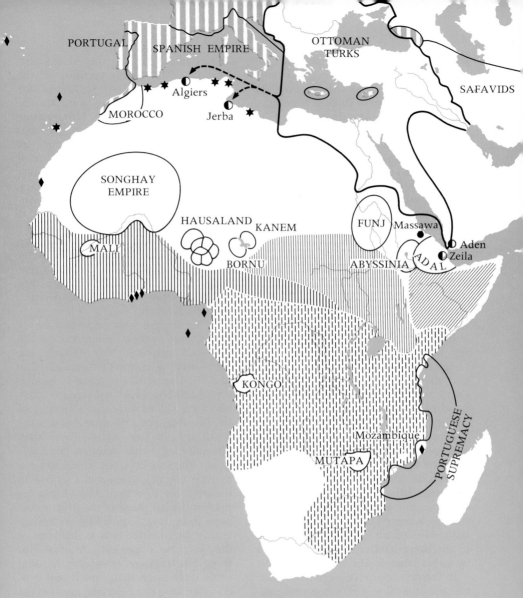

PORTUGAL SPANISH EMPIRE OTTOMAN
TURKS

SAFAVIDS

★ ★
Algiers
MOROCCO
Jerba

SONGHAY
EMPIRE

HAUSALAND KANEM
FUNJ Massawa
MALI BORNU Aden
ABYSSINIA Zeila
ADAL

KONGO

PORTUGUESE
SUPREMACY

Mozambique
MUTAPA

Islands and enclaves
♦ Portuguese
★ Spanish
☽ Ottoman

AD **1540**

THE Portuguese expedition to Abyssinia got off to a bad start, losing its commander and half its men in the course of its first campaign, but the next year it redeemed itself by winning a complete victory over the forces of the sultan of Adal. After this the Abyssinian king was able to recover his kingdom and there were still enough Portuguese left to sustain Abyssinia's military efficiency through the next generation. The Ottomans responded to this Christian success by occupying Massawa (1557), which cut the country off from further reinforcement. And in the Mediterranean the Turks had things all their own way, clearing the Spaniards from Tripolitania by 1551, from Algeria (bar Oran) by 1555 and from Tunisia by 1574.

In Black Africa Christianity had even less success. Though the king of the Kongo accepted baptism it couldn't be said that his kingdom ever became a Christian one: in the African manner the new beliefs were accepted as an addition to the native stock and not as an exclusive theology. Moreover the political tutelage that the Portuguese established over the kingdom proved of no use to either side. On the east coast the situation was different but the result much the same: the Arabs of the trading cities sullenly accepted Portuguese suzerainty but always remained Moslem: the Bantu in the hinterland remained untouched by either Islam or Christianity.

In fairness to the Portuguese it must be admitted that the resources committed by them were so small that it is hardly surprising that they had little impact. On the mainland, Portugal's sovereign possessions were limited to a few forts (Elmina plus Axim (built 1503) and Shama (1526) on the Akan coast, Luanda (1575) in the territory of the Ngola, Tete and Sena (1572) on the Zambesi and, the strong point for the East African protectorate, Mozambique (1508)), a commitment of perhaps 1,000 men in all. Traders and missionaries were, it is true, active at a number of points on the coast of Guinea and along the lower reaches of the Zaire and Zambesi, but here again the number involved in the sixteenth century is at most a thousand. The truth is that the voyages of discovery had opened up parts of the world that offered a better chance of a profit than Africa and that Portuguese energies were now diverted to these areas – to India, Indonesia, China and Japan.

In the interior some important movements came to their culmination in the sixteenth century. The Fulani, the cattle-herding nomads of Senegal who had been spreading eastward through the middle Niger region (as well as south into Futa Jallon) since the beginning of the fifteenth century, now reached the south side of Lake Chad. There they intermingled with another nomadic group, the Shuwa Arabs, who had been moving through the Sahel corridor in the opposite direction. The Shuwa represent the last phase of the Arab movement from Upper Egypt into the Sudan: it must be admitted that at this remove they were no longer very Arab in anything but language; they were herding cattle more often than camels and generally looking and behaving much as the local Nilo–Saharans. Finally, down at the southern end of the continent, the arrival of the Hereros in north-west Namibia marks the completion of the Bantu movement.

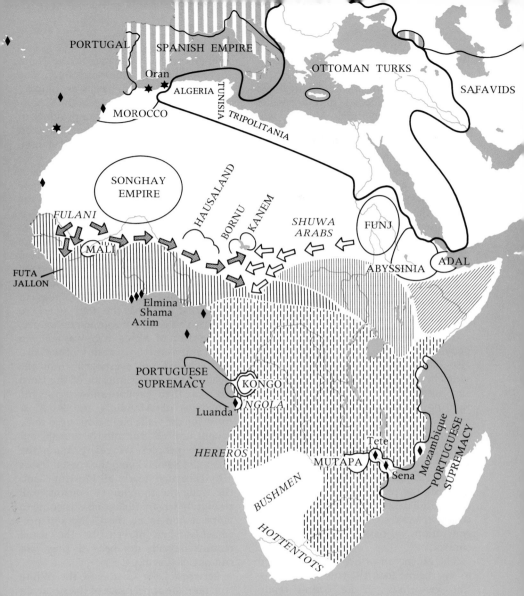

PORTUGAL

SPANISH EMPIRE

OTTOMAN TURKS

SAFAVIDS

Oran

ALGERIA

TUNISIA

TRIPOLITANIA

MOROCCO

FULANI

SONGHAY
EMPIRE

HAUSALAND

BORNU

KANEM

*SHUWA
ARABS*

FUNJ

ABYSSINIA

ADAL

MALI

FUTA
JALLON

Elmina
Shama
Axim

PORTUGUESE
SUPREMACY

KONGO

NGOLA

Luanda

HEREROS

MUTAPA

Tete

Sena

Mozambique

PORTUGUESE
SUPREMACY

BUSHMEN

HOTTENTOTS

Islands and enclaves
♦ Portuguese
★ Spanish

AD 1575

WHILE Spain and Turkey fought the big war in the Mediterranean Portugal and Morocco were locked into a smaller version of the same thing. Morocco was usually on the losing end of this because the Portuguese had control of the sea and could decide when and where to fight: as a result, through most of the sixteenth century Portugal controlled nearly as much of the Moroccan coastline as the Moroccans did. In 1578 the Portuguese attempted to improve on this situation: the biggest army they had ever sent overseas landed in Morocco with the king himself in command and a candidate for the Moroccan throne in tow. The idea was to make Morocco a satellite state and the hurry was to beat the Turks to it.

The outcome of the expedition was decided at the battle of Alcazar el Kebir, also known as the battle of the three kings because both the Portuguese king and his tame sultan were killed in the fighting and the sultan on the home side, already mortally ill, expired in the course of it. It was a disaster for the Portuguese: all but a handful of the 26,000 men in their army were either killed or captured. At a stroke Morocco acquired the prestige it needed to keep out of the Turkish embrace: Portugal, by contrast, was so shattered that for a generation it passed under Spanish control.

The Moroccan prince who succeeded to the throne took the title Almansur – 'the victorious'. If he hadn't really earned it yet he had every intention of doing so, and in 1590, against the unanimous advice of his cabinet, he organized a remarkable assault on the Songhay kingdom. For logistical reasons the expeditionary force had to be small: it numbered no more than 5,000 when it marched out of Marrakech in October 1590 and it was down to half this

strength when it arrived on the Niger four months later. This was enough. The feudal levy of Songhay was quickly dispersed by the musketry of the Moroccans, the kingdom became a province of Almansur's empire and the Moroccan exchequer was treated to a substantial injection of Sudanese bullion.

East Africa was also a busy place at this time. One movement brought a new wave of Nilo-Saharan pastoralists, the Luo, up the White Nile to the northern shore of Lake Victoria. Another, more dramatic one involved the Zimba, an outpouring of cannibal warriors from among the Maravi. The Zimba terrorized the coastal communities as far north as Malindi: it was their sack of Mombasa in 1589 that enabled the Portuguese to occupy this centre of Moslem resistance. In the Horn of Africa there was an even more important movement by the Galla: they fanned out westward from the Ogaden, the desert interior of the Horn that was their habitat, and overran the kingdoms of Abyssinia and Adal. A cause for the Galla migrations used to be sought in pressure from the Somali, but the two peoples are really much the same, the Somali being the coastal tribes – by this time nearly all Moslem – and the Galla the up-country cousins, still resolutely pagan. If anyone was going to move it had to be the Galla, and presumably they moved for the usual reasons nomads do, because they had run out of grazing.

Between Lake Chad and the White Nile note the appearance of the sultanate of Darfur: the sultans were Arab and Moslem; their Fur subjects, Nilo-Saharan and as yet uncertain of their commitment to Islam. In the Lake Chad area the big man now was Sultan Idris Aloma of Bornu: he had taken a leaf out of Almansur's book, recruited a corps of musketeers (in Tripoli) and used them to subdue Kanem.

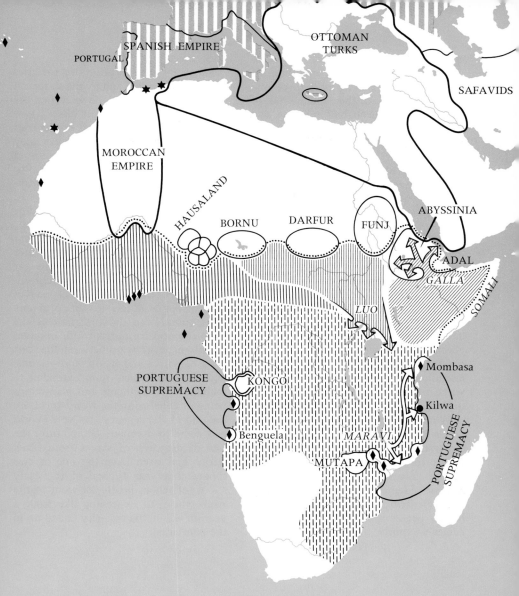

PORTUGAL

SPANISH EMPIRE

OTTOMAN
TURKS

SAFAVIDS

MOROCCAN
EMPIRE

HAUSALAND

BORNU

DARFUR

FUNJ

ABYSSINIA

ADAL

GALLA

SOMALI

LUO

PORTUGUESE
SUPREMACY

KONGO

Mombasa

Kilwa

Benguela

MARAVI

MUTAPA

PORTUGUESE
SUPREMACY

Islands and enclaves
♦ Portuguese
★ Spanish

AD 1600

BY 1600 the population of Africa had reached fifty-five million. Of this total eleven million, or one fifth, lived north of the Sahara — half of them in the Maghreb, half in Egypt. The remaining four fifths lived south of the Sahara, the major demographic focus being in West Africa though a secondary centre was forming in the region of modern Uganda, Rwanda and Burundi.

Most parts of Black Africa were now in some sort of contact with the outside world. The trade network built up by the Arabs in the medieval period served the Sahel, the northern Sudan and the east coast: the sea routes established by the Portuguese touched directly on the Atlantic communities and the peoples of present-day Mozambique and Rhodesia. The commodities most in demand in the Sahel and Sudan were salt, horses, cloth, glassware and metalware: on the sea coast the emphasis was on textiles, manufactures of various sorts and, later, when the taste for them had been acquired, alcohol and tobacco.

When it came to paying for these goods Black Africa had one thing everyone wanted, gold. It also had a surplus of slaves for sale: the Arab world was traditionally a big buyer of these, particularly of females for domestic service. Between them gold and slaves accounted for 90 per cent of the value of Black Africa's exports, the only other item of importance being ivory.

Slavery is an institution that societies seem to grow out of and by the sixteenth century Europe had done so. When the Portuguese tried to market black slaves there they found there was no demand for them and most of the slaves they bought in their early days were resold within Africa (mostly in Morocco). But then they found a use for slaves themselves. The Atlantic islands they had discovered in the course of their explorations — Madeira, the Cape Verde Isles, São Tomé and Principe — had turned out to be ideal for growing sugar cane, but, Europeans being reluctant to do this sort of work, the plantations were chronically short of labour. Black slaves provided a solution to the problem. Consequently, in the first half of the sixteenth century a brisk traffic in slaves (mostly male) grew up between the west coast of Africa and its offshore islands, and this traffic was soon extended to include the settlements and plantations being established in the New World. By the end of the century the New World had come to dominate the picture: the rate of despatch of slaves from Black Africa had risen from the one or two thousand a year typical of the early 1500s (of whom nearly all went to the Arab world) to something like 5,000 a year (of whom the majority ended up in the Americas).

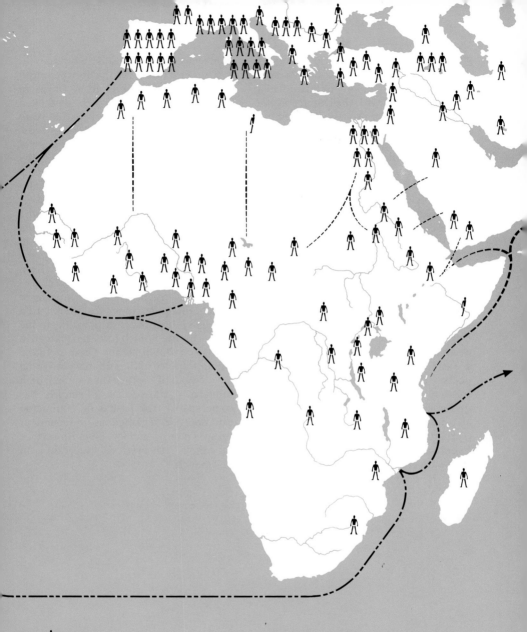

1 million people

**population and
trade routes in
AD 1600**

THE Spanish connection brought nothing but trouble for the Portuguese. The king of Spain had a standing quarrel with the Dutch and the Dutch were in the process of becoming the world's leading sea power. A more dangerous opponent for Portugal, with her fingertip hold on the African and Indian trades, can hardly be imagined. In 1637 a Dutch fleet took Elmina, within a few years the other posts on the Akan coast had gone too and the Portuguese found themselves completely shut out of the West African gold trade.

Nor was that all the bad news: both in the Far East and in Brazil the Portuguese empire was crumbling away under Dutch attack. In 1640 the Portuguese decided that they simply had to break with Spain and though doing so didn't bring an immediate end to their run of disasters – the next year the Dutch made a clean sweep of the African slaving ports – things did get better after that: by 1648 the resources had been scraped up for a counter-attack which recovered all three of the positions lost in 1641 (Fernando Po, Luanda and Benguela). Eventually Brazil was recovered too. In the South Atlantic at least, Portugal had managed to hang on to her empire.

The Dutch were not the only people to attack the Portuguese: from Oman in Arabia came a fleet which destroyed Portuguese hegemony over the Arab trading cities of the East African coast (1653). The Portuguese retained control over Mombasa, Mozambique and the posts to the south of Mozambique: in the interior their position was actually stronger, for they had achieved their longstanding ambition of establishing control over the kingdom of Mutapa (1633). There proved to be little profit in this: the gold it produced was only a fraction of the amount exported from West Africa.

Also worth a mention: the founding of revictualling stations for their East Indiamen – merchant ships sailing to the East – by the French (on Madagascar in 1642) and Dutch (at the Cape in 1652); the appearance of the sultanate of Wadai (an offshoot of Darfur); the way in which Morocco's trans-Saharan empire has come apart – the Pashas of Timbuctoo can now be regarded as independent princes paying no more than lip service to their theoretical suzerain in Marrakech.

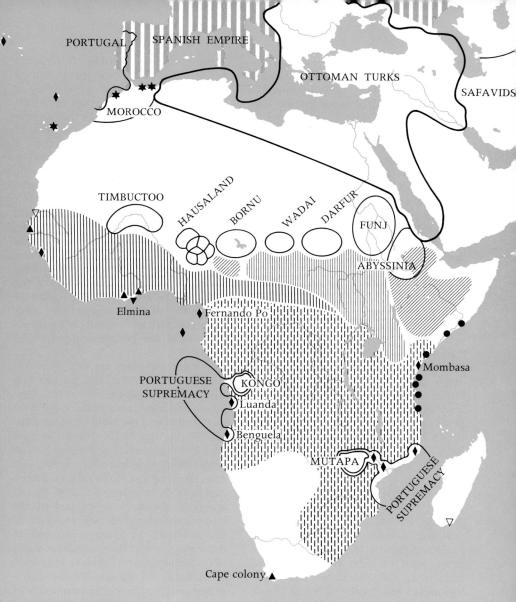

PORTUGAL   SPANISH EMPIRE

OTTOMAN TURKS

SAFAVIDS

MOROCCO

TIMBUCTOO

HAUSALAND   BORNU   WADAI   DARFUR   FUNJ

ABYSSINIA

Elmina

Fernando Po

Mombasa

PORTUGUESE
SUPREMACY

KONGO

Luanda

Benguela

MUTAPA

PORTUGUESE
SUPREMACY

Cape colony

Islands and enclaves

◆ Portuguese
★ Spanish
▲ Dutch
▽ French
▼ Danish

AD **1660**

BY the beginning of the eighteenth century it was clear that the Ottoman empire wasn't the power it had been a hundred years earlier. The African provinces had been allowed to drift into a state of near independence, with the authorities in Algiers, Tunis and Tripoli functioning more like sovereign governments than representatives of the sultan: in Egypt, though tribute was still remitted to Istanbul, the Mamluk nobles had won back much of their old power and ran the country pretty much as they pleased. The Sublime Porte – the Turkish government – seemed to have lost its ability or confidence, or both.

Western Europe, by contrast, was bursting with energy. As far as Africa is concerned the main result of this was the expansion of the Atlantic slave trade. By the early 1700s as many as 50,000 slaves were being shipped across the Atlantic every year, ten times as many as a century earlier. Nearly half of them were supplied by native dealers on the Bight of Benin, particularly its western sector, which came to be known as the 'Slave coast'. This was not chance: what is now southern Nigeria was the most populous part of Africa, and the Yoruba kingdom of Oyo, which had recently established control over a considerable part of it, provided the necessary organization.

Negro kingdoms perplexed Europeans, who tended to expect too much of them. Most of them were ceremonial rather than administrative units – they legitimized the local chiefs but didn't either appoint them or control them. Forcing kingdoms of this sort to make promises that they couldn't fulfil never did any good and sometimes caused their collapse. This is what happened to both the kingdom of the Kongo (which disintegrated completely in the late seventeenth century) and the kingdom of Mutapa (which was overthrown by a rival Shona kingdom, Butua, in 1693): indeed if the Portuguese had been able to establish themselves ashore in the Bight of Benin (which they couldn't because fevers killed them off too fast) the original kingdom they found there, centred on Benin city, would probably have gone the same way. As it was, the need for something capable of delivering the goods led to the appearance of the considerably more potent kingdom of Oyo – the effective demand of course being the African demand for European goods, not the European demand for slaves.

In West Africa note the French exploration of the Senegal (one of the few African rivers that can be readily navigated), the appearance of the English on the Gambia and the Gold coast, and the relative decline of the Dutch. In East Africa note that the Portuguese no longer hold Mombasa, which has just been taken by an Omani-led force after a desultory three-year siege (1696–8), but are now genuinely in control of the lower Zambesi region (the province of Mozambique). In Madagascar there is the appearance of the first native states of consequence (the Sakalava kingdoms of Menabe and Boina) and the disappearance of the French (a consequence of their success in colonizing the island of Réunion, 400 miles to the east).

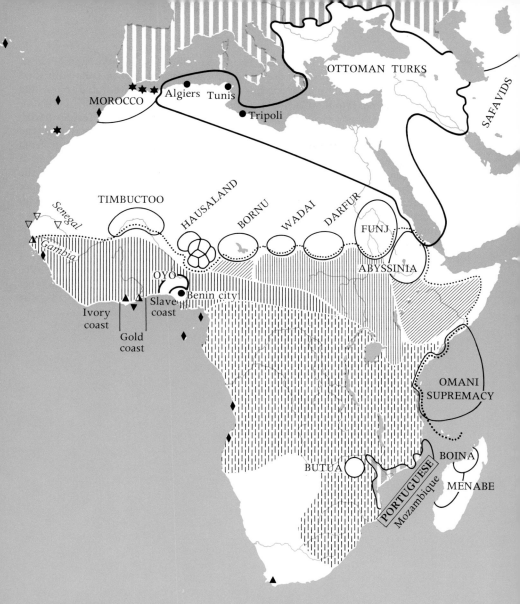

OTTOMAN TURKS

SAFAVIDS

MOROCCO
Algiers Tunis
Tripoli

Senegal
TIMBUCTOO
HAUSALAND
BORNU
WADAI
DARFUR
FUNJ
ABYSSINIA

Gambia

OYO
Benin city

Ivory
coast
Slave
coast
Gold
coast

OMANI
SUPREMACY

BUTUA

PORTUGUESE
Mozambique

BOINA

MENABE

Islands and enclaves
◆ Portuguese
★ Spanish
▲ Dutch
△ English
▽ French
▼ Danish

AD **1700**

THE first half of the eighteenth century was not a period of great change in Africa. In the north Algeria, Tunisia and Tripolitania finally established their complete independence of Ottoman Turkey (in 1710, 1705 and 1714 respectively). At the opposite end of the continent, in the Cape colony, some of the Boers (Dutch settlers) began to move inland, a process that led to a rapid decline in the numbers of the local Hottentots (a people of mixed Bushmen and Bantu ancestry) and the appearance of a new community, the Cape Coloureds (of Boer–Hottentot parentage). At the western end of the Sudan the decline of the Pashalik of Timbuctoo – now being regularly insulted by local Tuareg – was balanced by the rise of the Bambara, a Mande-speaking, traditionally animist people whose main town was Segu; at the eastern end a Funj sultan invaded Kordofan and incorporated it in his kingdom. The movement of Nilo-Saharans into East Africa resumed with the migrations of the Masai and the Tutsi. The Masai moved down from Lake Turkana through the highlands of Kenya to the Tanzanian steppe: the warrior Tutsi clans came from the upper White Nile to Rwanda and Burundi where they established themselves as a ruling caste over the local Bantu, the Hutu. On the Gold coast, in modern (but not ancient) Ghana, the Ashanti of Kumasi began to put together a supremacy over the Akan peoples that rivalled that of the kings of Oyo over the Yoruba.

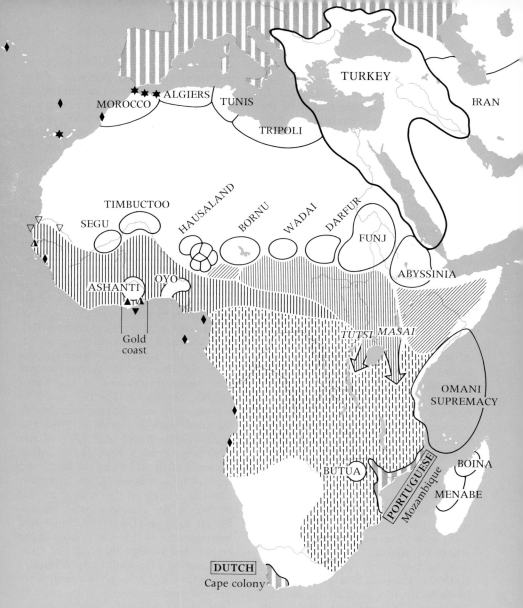

TURKEY

IRAN

MOROCCO

ALGIERS

TUNIS

TRIPOLI

TIMBUCTOO

SEGU

HAUSALAND

BORNU

WADAI

DARFUR

FUNJ

ABYSSINIA

ASHANTI

OYO

Gold
coast

TUTSI *MASAI*

OMANI
SUPREMACY

BOINA

BUTUA

PORTUGUESE

Mozambique

MENABE

DUTCH
Cape colony

Islands and enclaves

♦ Portuguese
✶ Spanish
▲ Dutch
△ British
▽ French
▼ Danish

AD **1750**

THE southern limit of Islam on this map shows little change from the position 100 years earlier. In the western Sudan the Fulani of the Senegal have made systematic use of the *jihad* to propagate the faith and in three areas, Futa Toro, Futa Jallon and Khasso, have succeeded in establishing theocratic states of a purity unusual in Black Africa (1776–86). On the Niger the trend is the other way: the disappearance of the Pashalik of Timbuctoo (it was extinguished by the Tuareg in 1787) has allowed the animist Bambara of Segu to extend their power down-river as far as this. In the rest of the Sudan there is nothing either way except that Kordofan, as a result of its conquest first by the Funj (c. 1750), then by Darfur (1790), is getting more Moslem.

By contrast the heartland of Islam in Africa, Egypt, is in ferment, a state of affairs induced by the arrival of Napoleon, his army (36,000 veterans of the French revolutionary wars) and his corps of savants (men of letters, men of science, mathematicians and engineers). Napoleon's announced mission was one of reform and according to him had the blessing of the Ottoman sultan and of the best Islamic theologians: if the background information was hardly correct the intention was firm: like it or not, reformed was what the Egyptians were going to be. Three weeks after stepping ashore (at Aboukir Bay, near Alexandria, in July 1798) Napoleon brushed aside the Mamluk host attempting to block his advance on Cairo (the so-called Battle of the Pyramids, though the fighting took place miles to the north of the pyramids) and made himself master of the country.

Exactly what the French hoped to do with Egypt in the long run is unclear: no one involved in the planning of the campaign seems to have thought beyond the short term. Napoleon was eager to play Alexander, his rivals were eager to see him out of France, the soldiers wanted to see the odalisques and do a bit of plundering. In fact, the French position wasn't really one that could be sustained for long because France's implacable enemy, Britain, had command of the sea. As soon as Admiral Nelson had found out what the French were up to he led the British Mediterranean Squadron into Aboukir Bay and battered Napoleon's fleet to bits. Napoleon stayed in Egypt a year more then slipped home on a frigate. What was left of his army followed him – under flag of truce – two years after that (September 1801).

By the third quarter of the eighteenth century the steady expansion of the Boers had brought them into contact with the southernmost of the Bantu peoples, the Xhosa. The first result of this was some skirmishes which, though dignified with the titles of First and Second Kaffir Wars (dated 1779–81 and 1793 respectively), were really only a matter of cattle raiding by the Xhosa and reprisal by the Boers. More important was the seizure of the colony by the British in the course of the Franco-British struggle (1795): the Dutch had been drawn into this war as allies of the French and though they got the Cape back during a brief lull in the hostilities (1803) they lost it for good shortly after the war was resumed – to be exact in 1806.

Note also the appearance of the first major Bantu kingdom in East Africa, the kingdom of Buganda on the north-west of Lake Victoria.

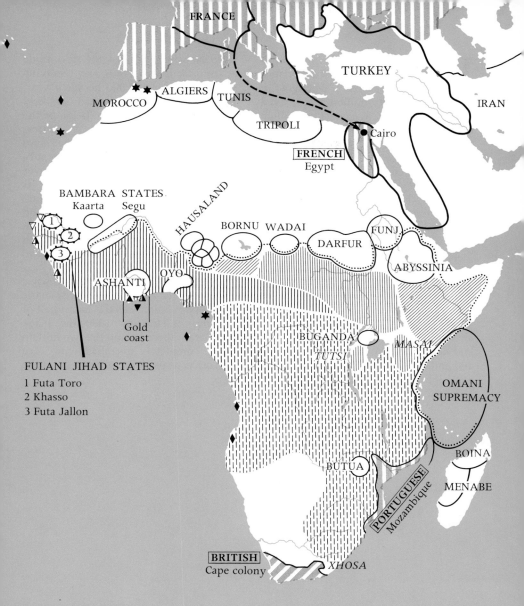

FRANCE

TURKEY

IRAN

MOROCCO

ALGIERS

TUNIS

TRIPOLI

Cairo

FRENCH
Egypt

BAMBARA STATES
Kaarta   Segu

HAUSALAND

BORNU WADAI

DARFUR

FUNJ

ABYSSINIA

1

2

3

ASHANTI

OYO

Gold
coast

FULANI JIHAD STATES

1 Futa Toro
2 Khasso
3 Futa Jallon

BUGANDA

TUTSI

MASAI

OMANI
SUPREMACY

BUTUA

BOINA

MENABE

PORTUGUESE
Mozambique

BRITISH
Cape colony

XHOSA

Islands and enclaves

♦ Portuguese
✱ Spanish
▲ Dutch
△ British
▽ French
▼ Danish

AD **1800**

BY the beginning of the nineteenth century Black Africa's dominance of the continent's demography was absolute: sixty million people lived south of the Sahara as against ten million to the north of it. True, the sub-Saharan total includes about five million Cushites, who are not strictly speaking black, and 1.5 million Malagasy, who are not black at all, but nonetheless Africa was now clearly the black man's domain: three out of every four people living there were either Negro or Nilo-Saharan.

Exchanges with the outside world had no effect on this situation, though they did have marked consequences for the demography of the Americas. The Black Africans taken as slaves to the New World created a community there that already numbered five million in 1800 and can be estimated at something like 100 million today. That this enforced exodus had no effect at all on Africa may seem surprising because the slave trade at its peak in the 1780s was removing something near 100,000 people a year. However, this is less than half the likely rate of increase for a population of the size existing in Black Africa at the time and the fact that a majority of the slaves were male means that the effective subtraction was smaller than this. Moreover the Atlantic traffic was not without its advantages: in particular the introduction of new staples like manioc and maize may well have produced an increase in the rate of population growth that outweighed the loss due to the slave trade.

One place where the spread of maize growing is certainly linked to a dramatic rise in population was the Bantu half of southern Africa. By 1800 the black population there was on the two million mark, completely overshadowing – in numerical terms – the 16,000 Boers of the Cape.

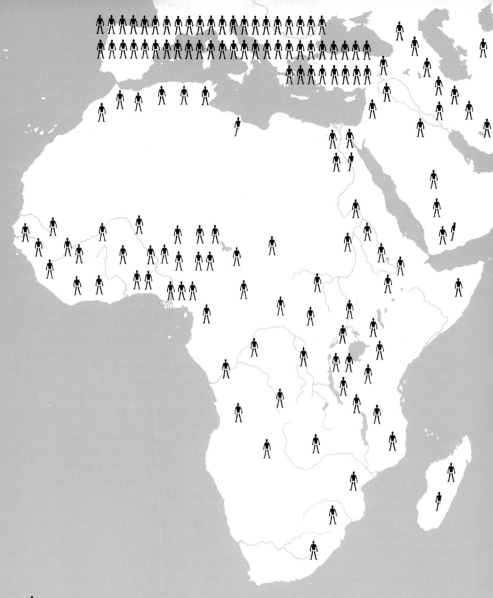

$\stackrel{\text{人}}{\text{八}}$ 1 million people

population in
AD **1800**

AS far as Europe was concerned, Black Africa remained an unknown continent for an astonishing length of time. South of a line drawn through Lake Chad, less than a quarter of the land could be mapped with any confidence in the year 1800: how the Nile began, how the Niger ended and where the Zaire came from remained entirely mysterious.

There was a simple reason for this: malaria. If ten Europeans landed in West Africa it was pretty well certain that six of them would be dead – nearly all of malaria – before a year was out. And inland, mortality was even fiercer. Not for nothing was West Africa known as the White Man's Grave.

With such powerful reasons as this for not stepping ashore it is no wonder that the European kept his contact with Africa to a minimum. The Africans brought their commodities – slaves, ivory or gold – to the coast; the Europeans traded as much as they could from their ships. To promote and protect this trade it was sometimes necessary to maintain establishments ashore, but when this was done it was done reluctantly and more often to block access by other Europeans than to gain control over Africans.

The exception to this generalization is the Cape. The colony there was healthy and grew vigorously. Boer farmers soon explored the hinterland and by 1800 had reconnoitred as far as the Orange River. The Portuguese had also got something to show in Angola and Mozambique though this was because they had by this time been there so long – nearly 300 years – that they had had time to breed a disease-resistant Afro-Portuguese population that could survive in the interior. Even so, the two settlements remained almost entirely littoral and if their trading networks stretched up to 400 miles inland, there was still another 800 miles of completely unexplored territory between them. An attempt to cross this gap by Francisco Lacerda in 1798 ended in his death at the *kraal* of Cazembe, the furthest inland of the native chiefs that the Portuguese traders on the Zambesi had had dealings with.

Some idea of the odds facing the would-be explorer of Africa at this time can be gained from the expeditions of Mungo Park. He set out from England in 1795 to find out what he could about the Niger and despite bouts of fever was able to make his way from the Gambia to Segu in the course of 1796. There he turned back because it was quite clear that he would be killed if he tried to go further: the Moslems of the middle Niger were implacably hostile to Christians. In 1805 he tried again: this time he had with him a company of British soldiers. The idea was to buy a boat at Segu, get it into midstream and sail down to the sea without putting foot to shore again: anyone who tried to stop them would have to argue with four dozen muskets, an immense concentration of firepower by local standards. It was a perfectly feasible plan except that few Europeans had Park's resistance to malaria. The soldiers died like flies on the march to Segu and by the time Park had got his boat launched only four of the expedition's forty-six members were still alive. Nevertheless Park successfully navigated his way along a thousand miles of the river: it was only when he was caught at the Bussa rapids that he and the remainder of his company succumbed to an attack – ironically enough by non-Moslems who thought he was a Moslem invader. His death left it uncertain whether the Niger emerged where it does – the delta that in the nineteenth century was usually referred to as the Oil rivers – or curved south on a wider radius and became the Zaire, or turned back north to end in L. Chad.

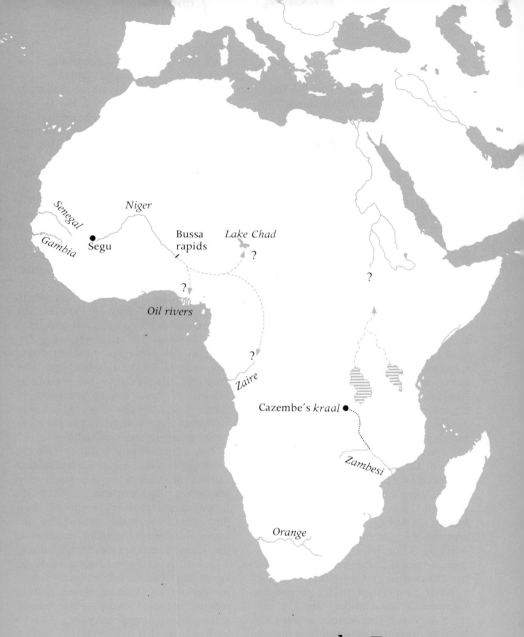

Senegal

Niger

Gambia

Segu

Bussa
rapids

Lake Chad

?

?

?

Oil rivers

?

Zaire

Cazembe's *kraal*

Zambesi

Orange

**the European
geographer's
view of Africa in
AD 1800**

IN the 1820s the mounting population pressure in the black half of South Africa caused an outburst of political violence, the *mfecane* or 'time of troubles'. At the eye of the storm was the dreaded Shaka, king of the Zulus from 1818 to 1828. His reign was an endless series of battles which, because he trained his *impis* (regiments) to use their spears for stabbing instead of throwing, he nearly always won: his leadership transformed the Zulu, who had previously been a relatively unimportant clan, into the master race of the south-east.

To stand against a Zulu onslaught was to invite disaster: by the mid-1820s most of Shaka's nearer neighbours were trying to put as much space between themselves and Zululand as possible. Some tribes fled south, but British troops were now holding the eastern frontier of the Cape colony and there was little hope of breaking this line (along the Great Fish river) or being allowed to settle within the colony even if they did. Others went north, into what is now Mozambique, but this is not a very welcoming part of the world and only a few small groups made a success of this move. The best line of retreat proved to be through the Drakensberg – the mountain range that parallels the coast – and onto the High Veld. This had previously been a quiet part of Africa, thinly populated by outlying Sotho tribes (the main Sotho groups occupied the western slopes of the Drakensberg): the arrival of Nguni bands (Nguni is the term for the peoples between the Drakensberg and the sea: their distinguishing feature is that they have incorporated clicks in their speech as a result of contact with the Hottentots) threw the whole area into anarchy.

In West Africa the opening years of the nineteenth century saw a continuation of the Fulani *jihads* that marked the last quarter of the eighteenth. The most spectacular was launched in 1804 by Usman dan Fodio, a Fulani of Hausaland. Within a few years he had made himself master of all the Hausa city states: he then enlarged the area of his control to include the surrounding communities. In doing so he enlarged the definition of Hausaland, which now came to mean not just the seven city states but the seven adjacent districts as well. One of them was Ilorin, previously the northern province of the Yoruba empire of Oyo: following the loss of Ilorin the Oyo hegemony collapsed, leaving one of its client states, Dahomey, as the only kingdom of any moment between Hausaland and the sea.

Usman dan Fodio died at his newly built capital of Sokoto in 1817. He left his empire to his capable son Mohamed Bello. He also left an enterprising disciple in the person of Ahmadu Lobo, who moved to the middle Niger and preached the *jihad* to the Fulani of Masina. Ahmadu was so successful in this that within a few years he had won control of the whole stretch of the river between Jenne and Timbuctoo.

Two other empire builders were at work at the same time. One was Radama I, king of Merina in the interior of Madagascar. In his brief reign (1810–28) he expanded the very moderate-sized (but populous) state created by his father into the dominating kingdom of the island. The other was Mohamed Ali, a Turkish general sent to restore order in Egypt after the French withdrew. And Mohamed Ali deserves more than a passing mention because he, almost alone among contemporary African leaders, saw that achieving the sort of military superiority enjoyed by the French was not just a matter of buying in European firearms, it meant altering the social structure of the army.

Mohamed Ali's reforms can be said to have begun in 1811, when he invited the

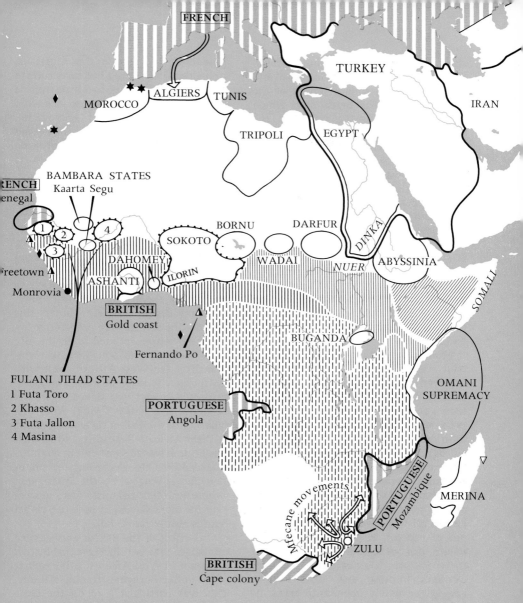

FRENCH

TURKEY

IRAN

MOROCCO ALGIERS TUNIS

TRIPOLI EGYPT

FRENCH
Senegal

BAMBARA STATES
Kaarta Segu

BORNU DARFUR

DINKA

ABYSSINIA

1
2   4
3

SOKOTO WADAI

NUER

SOMALI

Freetown

Monrovia

DAHOMEY
ASHANTI ILORIN

BRITISH
Gold coast

BUGANDA

Fernando Po

FULANI JIHAD STATES
1 Futa Toro
2 Khasso
3 Futa Jallon
4 Masina

OMANI
SUPREMACY

PORTUGUESE
Angola

Mfecane movements

PORTUGUESE
Mozambique

MERINA

ZULU

BRITISH
Cape colony

Islands and enclaves
♦ Portuguese
★ Spanish
▲ British
▽ French

AD 1830

surviving members of the Mamluk leadership to a banquet in Cairo and massacred them. This disposed of the last remnants of this feudal caste which had claimed exclusive rights to the profession of arms in Egypt. He then proceeded to recruit from the despised peasantry of the country an infantry force which was equipped and trained to fight Western style. When the Ottoman sultan appealed for help in dealing with a rebellion in Arabia, Mohamed Ali's new model army was able to succeed where old style Turkish forces had failed. By 1818 he had restored order in Arabia: in 1820 he launched a campaign on his own account against Nubia. This was rapidly pushed through to complete success, creating an Egyptian empire that outclassed anything the pharaohs had achieved.

Mohamed Ali's reforms were civil as well as military: he built schools by the hundred and created new administrative departments by the dozen: he took a census and set up a government printing press. The difficulty that he didn't really solve was how to pay for it all. Egypt's wealth remained purely agricultural, indeed the gap between the industrial performance of the country and that of Europe actually widened during his reign. This meant that the import bill was always threatening to get out of control. Hopes that the Sudan would turn out to be rich in gold proved to be without foundation and though elephant hunting and slave raiding among the newly opened-up areas inhabited by the Dinka and Nuer peoples on the White Nile produced some extra revenue, none of the newly won provinces ever repaid the cost of conquest.

On the east coast of Africa the energetic Sultan Sayyid of Oman started to turn his suzerainty over the coastal cities into an effective sovereignty (from 1813 on). In the north the French sent an expedition to chastise the Algerians, whom they considered had been rude to their ambassador: they had little trouble occupying the town and little idea what to do with it once they had (1830). Tripoli occupied the oases of the Fezzan in an attempt to gain control of the trade on the Tripoli–Bornu route, now at its busiest ever (1811).

The opening decade of the nineteenth century saw the first effective moves made to end the Atlantic slave trade. The leading role was taken by the British, who outlawed the slave trade in their dominions in 1807 and then began to bully the other European powers into doing the same. Of course, passing laws against the slave trade was one thing, enforcing them another, but in this instance the British were prepared to lay out the resources needed to do the job: from 1808 a naval squadron was stationed on the West African coast with instructions to stop and search any ship suspected of carrying slaves regardless of whose flag it was flying. From this time on, the number of slaves carried out of West Africa fell steadily and though this decline was to some extent counterbalanced by a rise in the number smuggled out of Angola by the Portuguese (whose Brazilian colonists were always avid for more slaves) in time the global figures also began to fall.

One effect of the British anti-slavery campaign was an increase in British influence in West Africa relative to that of the other European trading nations. This was particularly so on the Gold coast, which, though it still had as many Dutch and Danish forts as British, now became for all practical purposes a British protectorate. The decisive step was taken in 1824, when troops were committed to 'liberate' the Fante tribes of the coast from the rule of the Ashantehene (king of Ashanti): after an initial disaster in the best traditions of the British army, this was duly done. Strictly speaking this map and the next should still show Danish installations on the Gold coast (the Danes sold out to the British only in 1850), and this and the next two, Dutch ones (the Dutch hung on till 1872), but marking the coastline as British-controlled seems a better rendering of the political reality; Dutch and Danish interest was by this stage purely commercial.

The British Gold Coast Colony (officially instituted in 1874) eventually evolved into present-day Ghana. Two other West African countries, Sierra Leone and Liberia, have an early history that has even closer links with the anti-slavery movement. Freetown, the original nucleus of Sierra Leone, was founded by the British in 1792 as a refuge for North American slaves who had chosen the British side in the American War of Independence and had subsequently been languishing in the bleaker climate of Canada. However, no more than 1,000 of these unfortunate 'loyalists' ever arrived at Freetown, and the future of the colony was very much in doubt when the Royal Navy's anti-slavery squadron arrived there in 1808. This proved to be the turning point. The navy rescued a lot of people from the holds of the slavers they intercepted – about 100,000 in all over the next fifty odd years – and it landed 80 per cent of them at Freetown. Half of them tried to get back to their original homes (very few can have succeeded), but half of them stayed: they were settlers who made Freetown a success.

Monrovia, the capital of Liberia, has a rather similar history. Founded in 1821 by an American charity helping freed slaves to return to Africa, most of its citizens did in fact come from across the Atlantic – in sum about 16,000 by the time Liberia was constituted as an independent republic (1847). Involuntary settlers – in this case the product of the US navy's anti-slavery patrols – amounted to 6,000 or so. Of course all these figures are small: the immigrants were never more than a drop in the local bucket and only 1 per cent of present-day Liberians, for example, claim an Afro-American ancestry. They run the country, though.

In 1827, in order to monitor the traffic off the Slave Coast more effectively, the Royal Navy established a base on Fernando Po. This island had been ceded by Portugal to Spain in 1776 in return for Spanish cessions in South America: now it was leased to Britain by Spain and remained under British control till 1858. During this period the anti-slavery squadron finally gained the upper hand over the Atlantic slavers and an end was put to the export of Africans to the Americas.

No one in Africa was going to say thank you for this. Most West African states suffered a severe loss of revenue and, though the British granted some of them subsidies in compensation and, in the case of the principalities of the Niger delta, went to considerable trouble to encourage the production of palm oil as an alternative source of income, this was a period of relative impoverishment all along Africa's Atlantic seaboard. Even the various categories of people who had supplied the slave trade with its raw material can't be said to have benefited: criminals were once again handed over to the civil executioner and prisoners-of-war to the witch-doctors for sacrifice. This is the reason why the accounts of West African kingdoms in the nineteenth century are so blood-curdling: states like Dahomey that had built up a big slave-exporting capacity now had to consume a lot of unwanted human beings. Their ways of doing so provide a last bizarre flourish to what had always been a sad and sorry business.

THE Boers, who had never liked the governors sent out by the Dutch, liked the ones the British sent even less. At a time when public opinion in Europe had swung decisively against slavery the Boers remained wedded to their view of the native African as an inferior being created by God to toil for the white man. The British governors, under instructions from home to liberalize the Cape Colony and under pressure from the local missionaries to do something more than window dressing, tried to get the Boers to keep their brutalities within bounds. Outraged, the Boers determined to leave. Between 1835 and 1840 some 10,000 of them crossed the Orange River, the effective limit of British jurisdiction, and moved onto the High Veld.

The leaders of this 'Great Trek' wanted to set up an independent Boer state with its own access to the sea. While some of the Trekkers settled the High Veld, Piet Retief led the main group east through the Drakensberg into Natal. Natal was a Zulu borderland and the Zulu King Dingane (Shaka's half-brother, murderer and successor) had no scruple about massacring Retief and his entourage when they visited his *kraal*: however, the Boers had the better of the fighting that followed and in 1839 the Trekkers were finally able to proclaim the independent republic they had always wanted.

Meanwhile the tribes dispersed in the *mfecane* were nearing their final destinations. The largest group, the Ngoni, settled either side of Lake Nyasa after inflicting weakening defeats on the Shona (of present-day Rhodesia) and the Maravi (of present-day Malawi). A Sotho group, the Makololo, conquered the Lozi kingdom of Barotse on the upper Zambesi, which is why the area is Sotho-speaking today. And the Ndebele, spurred on their way by the Trekkers, overthrew the crumbling kingdom of the western Shona, Butua, and established their own rule in its place. The social hierarchy they instituted is a synopsis of their history: the Nguni speakers, the nuclear group in the *mfecane* dispersal, became the ruling caste; the Sotho-speaking followers they had acquired during the passage across the High Veld ranked second and the basal Shona population formed the third and lowest stratum.

The French, unable to make up their minds to leave Algeria, attempted to conquer the country and by 1840 had succeeded as far as the maritime regions were concerned. However, they were unable to impose their rule on the tribes of the Atlas, who found a doughty leader in the person of Abd el-Kader. The Ottomans re-established direct control over Tripoli in 1835, though they didn't occupy the Fezzan oases until 1842. Sultan Sayyid of Oman completed the pacification of the African end of his empire and, finding it much richer than the Arabian end, moved his court to Zanzibar (1840). Mohamed Ali reluctantly gave up his attempt to take over the whole Ottoman empire when the European powers, particularly the British, made it clear that they weren't going to let him do it (1830–40).

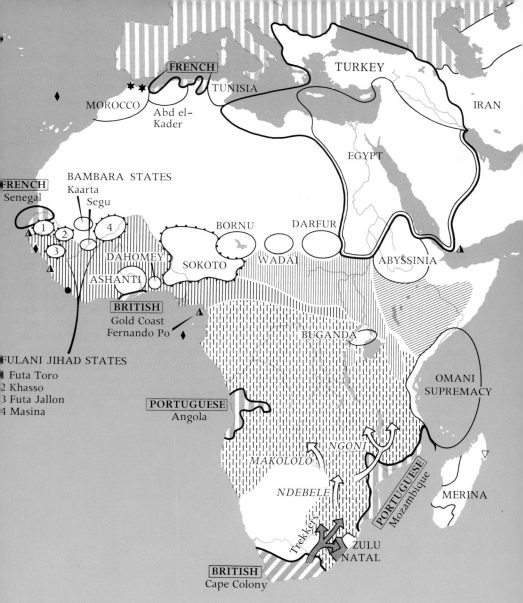

FRENCH
MOROCCO
Abd el-Kader
TUNISIA
TURKEY
IRAN
EGYPT

FRENCH
Senegal

BAMBARA STATES
Kaarta
Segu

1
2
4
3

BORNU
DARFUR
ABYSSINIA

DAHOMEY
SOKOTO
WADAI

ASHANTI

BRITISH
Gold Coast
Fernando Po

FULANI JIHAD STATES
1 Futa Toro
2 Khasso
3 Futa Jallon
4 Masina

BUGANDA

OMANI
SUPREMACY

PORTUGUESE
Angola

NGONI

MAKOLOLO

NDEBELE

PORTUGUESE
Mozambique

MERINA

Trekkers
ZULU
NATAL

BRITISH
Cape Colony

Islands and enclaves
♦ Portuguese
✹ Spanish
▲ British
▽ French

AD **1840**

CONTINUING trouble between the Boers of Natal and the local Bantu led to British intervention in 1842: eventually Natal was made a British colony and most of the Boers left. They trekked back through the Drakensberg and on to the High Veld, which now became the last redoubt of the Boer way of life. This time the British accepted the Boers' right to exist: they officially recognized the independence of the Transvaal Boers in 1852 and of the Orange Free State in 1854.

The resistance of the Algerians to the French occupation of their country was broken by General Bugeaud's campaigns in 1841–7. The end came with the surrender of Abd el-Kader in 1847 and thereafter European settlers began to move into the country in increasing numbers. Only a minority were French. Most were Spanish, Italian or Maltese: by 1856 there were 170,000 of them. This is almost exactly the same as the figure for whites in South Africa (140,000 in the Cape, 30,000 in the Boer republics, 7,500 in Natal), the only other population of European origin in the continent to have reached a significant size. The next in line would be the 3,000 or so Portuguese in Angola and Mozambique.

The French were also instituting a forward policy in Senegal. This brought them into conflict with al-Hajj Umar, the leader of the last of the Fulani *jihads* and the conqueror of Kaarta. The result was a stand-off: al-Hajj Umar didn't manage to take the new fort the French had built at Medina but the French didn't try to advance beyond this point.

Zanzibar and Oman split into two separate sultanates on the death of Sultan Sayyid in 1856. The French put garrisons on to the islands of Mayotte in the Comoros and Nosy Bé off Madagascar in 1841. The rise of the Sanusi brotherhood, now becoming the dominant force in the life of the bedouin of the central Sahara, is associated with the opening of a new trade route running from Benghazi in Cyrenaica to Wadai in the Sudan.

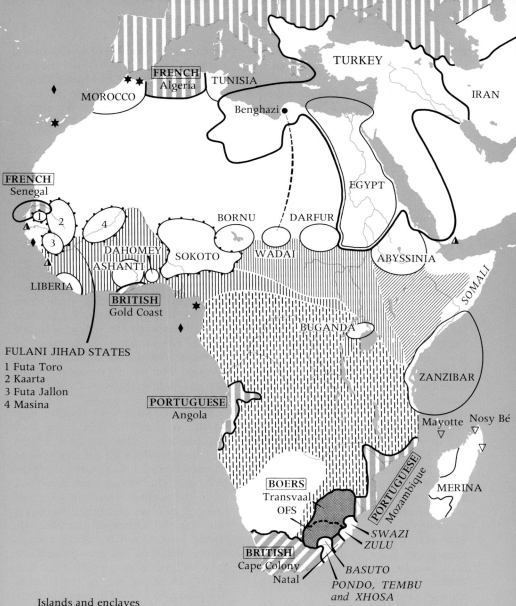

TURKEY

IRAN

FRENCH
Algeria   TUNISIA

MOROCCO

Benghazi

EGYPT

FRENCH
Senegal

① ② ④

③

DAHOMEY
ASHANTI

BORNU   DARFUR

SOKOTO   WADAI

ABYSSINIA

SOMALI

LIBERIA

BRITISH
Gold Coast

BUGANDA

FULANI JIHAD STATES

1 Futa Toro
2 Kaarta
3 Futa Jallon
4 Masina

ZANZIBAR

PORTUGUESE
Angola

Mayotte   Nosy Bé
▽   ▽

MERINA

BOERS
Transvaal
OFS

PORTUGUESE
Mozambique

SWAZI
ZULU

BRITISH
Cape Colony
Natal

BASUTO

PONDO, TEMBU
and XHOSA

Islands and enclaves

♦   Portuguese
★   Spanish
▲   British
▽   French

AD **1856**

THE problem of where the Niger emerged was finally solved by the Lander brothers, who travelled overland from the Guinea coast to the Bussa rapids (where Mungo Park had been killed) and sailed down from there to the sea (1830–32). There was still a certain amount of confusion about the Niger's main tributary, the Benue, which it was thought might arise from Lake Chad: this was sorted out by Heinrich Barth, who showed that it didn't and that the Chari–Chad system was a closed one.

On the other side of the continent Mohamed Ali was tackling the problem of the Nile: a series of expeditions up-river from Khartoum succeeded in penetrating the Sudd and mapping the White Nile as far as the cataract above Juba (1839–42). This meant that the course of the river was now known to within a few hundred miles of its traditional source, the East African lakes. And considerably more was known about these. Arab slavers from Zanzibar were regularly visiting Ujiji on Lake Tanganyika and had brought back reports of two other big lakes, Ukerewe to the north and Nyasa to the south. Because only their nearer shores were known with any certainty some maintained – and this was the view favoured by the local Europeans – that all three were part of a single vast inland sea, the Unyamwezi. Whether this was true or not it seemed that 'Lake Nyasa' was the same body of water as the Portuguese on the Zambesi had had reports of under the name of Lake Maravi.

The Zambesi itself was mapped out by David Livingstone, a missionary with little stomach for ordinary mission work but a burning desire to see Africa opened up and brought into the community of nations. His account of his crossing of the continent in 1855–6 – not the first, but the first anyone had heard about – was an instant best-seller in Britain: it persuaded the British government to provide him with the money he needed to continue his work.

The British government was already into African exploration in a small way, for it had agreed to subsidize Burton and Speke's expedition to the East African lakes. Burton was a traveller rather than an explorer – in the course of a long life of journeying he visited and documented such diverse places as Mecca, Dahomey and Salt Lake City – and he was an Arabist rather than an Africanist, but as the plan on this occasion was simply to use the Arab slaving route from Zanzibar to Ujiji on Lake Tanganyika, his qualities seemed entirely appropriate to the job in hand. Speke was by comparison a one-idea man: he was obsessed with finding the source of the Nile and nothing else was of real interest to him.

Burton and Speke got on well enough on the way to Ujiji but when they arrived there Speke was upset to find Lake Tanganyika a bit too low-lying to fit easily into what was known about the Nile basin. On the way back he slipped off to the north in search of Ukerewe, found it and was instantly certain that this was the source of the Nile. He rushed back to tell Burton of his discovery, which he had proudly renamed Lake Victoria. Burton pointed out that Speke's three-day stay at the lakeside had produced no evidence except hearsay for the lake being unusually large and no evidence at all that it had anything to do with the Nile. By the time they reached Zanzibar the two were no longer talking to each other.

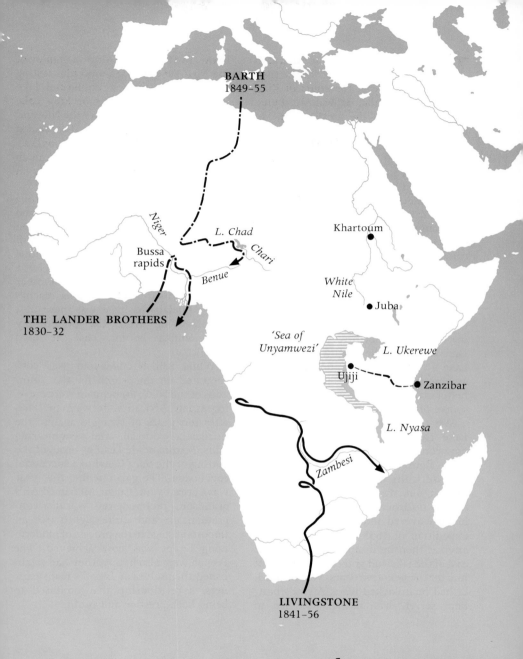

BARTH
1849–55

Niger

**Bussa
rapids**

L. Chad

Chari

Khartoum

Benue

*White
Nile*

• Juba

THE LANDER BROTHERS
1830–32

'Sea of
Unyamwezi'

L. Ukerewe

Ujiji

• Zanzibar

L. Nyasa

Zambesi

LIVINGSTONE
1841–56

the European
view of Africa in
AD 1856

IN 1860 Speke was back in Africa: in 1862, after a somewhat longer than intended stay at the court of King Mutesa of Buganda, he was surveying the Rippon Falls, the great cascade in which Lake Victoria gives birth to the Nile. Lake Victoria *was* as big as he said it was – and it *was* the source of the world's longest and most famous river. He travelled north a happy man.

At Gondokoro he met Mr and Mrs Samuel Baker, who had come south from Khartoum to meet him. He told the Bakers of his discovery and also of rumours of a lake that apparently lay to the west of Lake Victoria. In 1864 the Bakers reached this lake, which they named Lake Albert, and found that Speke's Nile – the Victoria Nile – flowed into its north-east corner: the Nile proper began at its north-west corner. So if Lake Albert reached further south than Lake Victoria – and it could do so for all anyone knew – then it would have a better claim than Lake Victoria to be the source of the Nile. Poor Speke!

What with Burton still arguing for Lake Tanganyika, public interest was now considerable, and Livingstone, the father figure of African exploration, had little difficulty in funding an expedition to sort out the problem. In 1866 he moved up from Lake Nyasa (which he had discovered and explored during his expedition of 1858–63) to Lake Tanganyika: then he disappeared off to the east of the lake and nothing was heard of him for the next five years. Was he dead, or had he unlocked Black Africa's best-kept secret? The newspapers had to know. In 1871 Henry Morton Stanley of the *New York Herald* found him resting up at Ujiji, battered but not beaten. Like Burton, Livingstone was backing Lake Tanganyika as the source of the Nile and he had found out something that seemed to support the idea: Lake Tanganyika's outlet, the Lualaba River, ran as much north as west; this could be the Nile on its way to Lake Albert.

Together Stanley and Livingstone proved that Lake Tanganyika had no other outlet than the Lualaba: then Stanley set off back to Zanzibar full of plans and inspiration. Livingstone wouldn't come with him, wouldn't leave Africa. In 1872 he started out on another journey, this time to the upper reaches of the Lualaba basin: it was there, at a spot not far from the present-day Zaire–Zambia border, that he died (1873).

While British endeavour was concentrated on the search for the 'fountains of the Nile', Frenchmen were creating a new African waterway. In 1869, after ten years of struggle against the financial, political and engineering odds, Ferdinand de Lesseps brought the cutting of the Suez Canal to a successful conclusion. The gala opening that year was a great event. Ismail, Mohamed Ali's grandson, received the world's congratulations and quite rightly so: an important stage in the process of modernizing Egypt was now achieved. The French were also happy: they had established themselves as Ismail's main partners, a relationship that promised to bring both prestige and profit.

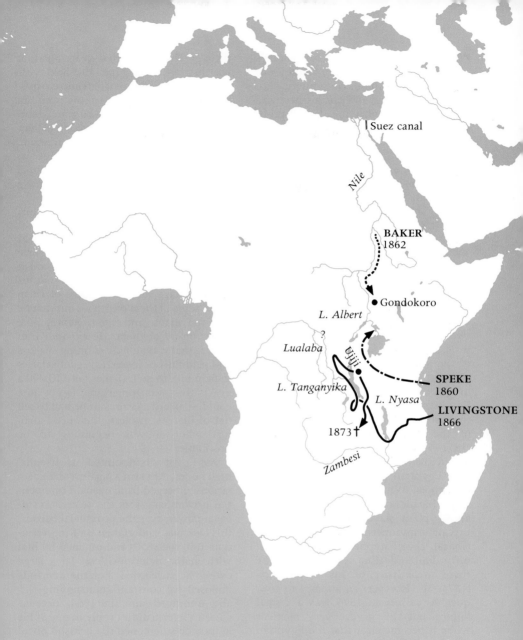

Suez canal

Nile

BAKER
1862

● Gondokoro

L. Albert

Lualaba

Ujiji

SPEKE
1860

L. Tanganyika

L. Nyasa

LIVINGSTONE
1866

1873 †

Zambesi

European exploration
of the East African Lakes
AD 1860–73

THE year after Livingstone's death Henry Morton Stanley was back in Africa. He brought with him the resources, the ruthlessness and the organizing ability to solve all problems. First he circumnavigated Lake Victoria (1875), then Lake Tanganyika (1876). Then, in the most staggering single episode in the history of African exploration, he launched himself and his steel boat, the *Lady Alice*, on to the Lualaba and toiled and fought his way downstream to reach the sea in August 1877. The Lualaba was the Zaire, Lake Victoria was the source of the Nile.

As far as the political map of Africa is concerned the most important development during this period is the expansion of Egypt. Ismail, who ruled the country from 1863 to 1879, sent expeditions in two directions: down the Red Sea (a programme associated with the cutting of the Suez Canal) and up the Nile. In 1865 he persuaded the Ottoman sultan to place Suakin and Massawa under Egyptian control: he then put garrisons in most of the ports on the African side of the Red Sea and Gulf of Aden (1871–5). As for the Sudan he hired Samuel Baker, the explorer, to set up a new Egyptian province, Equatoria, on the upper White Nile (1871–3). And when Darfur was conquered by Zubair, an Egyptian slave trader who had a private army operating on the Bahr al-Ghazal, Ismail stepped in and by some nifty double dealing was able to make these areas part of his empire too (1874–5). However, an attempt to conquer Abyssinia in 1875 was a dismal failure and this at the very moment when it became clear that the Egyptian treasury was in desperate trouble. What had gone wrong? What was Ismail to do for money?

What Ismail did was to sell his 44 per cent interest in the Suez Canal to the British for £4 million, which saw him through the rest of that year. But that was his last asset gone: the next year brought – besides more defeats in Abyssinia – national bankruptcy and an ultimatum from the European debt-holders as a result of which control over the Egyptian budget passed to them. Egypt entered the first stage of its colonial bondage – a sort of international protectorate – without a shot being fired.

Ismail has been much blamed for this, and not without reason. His way of solving problems was to throw money at them, which is fair enough for a prince of the blood in private life but no good at all on a national scale. It wasn't that his ideas weren't sensible – some of them were, some of them weren't – but that he had too many and spent money like water on all of them. He expanded an empire that was already running at a loss and paid Europeans extravagant salaries to help him to do it (Baker got £10,000 a year): this was something Egypt just couldn't afford. As a result he had to sell out of his best project, the Suez Canal, just when it was beginning to be profitable.

As Egypt disappointed its friends' high hopes, Abyssinia, against all expectations, emerged from chaos. The essential preliminary was the restoration of royal power over the provincial barons: this task was undertaken by King Theodore II in the 1850s and pursued by him with manic determination. To a large extent he succeeded, but the demands imposed by constant campaigning finally unhinged him; in 1864, because Queen Victoria didn't reply to one of his letters, he summoned the British Consul before him, put him in irons and incarcerated him in the fortress of Magdala. To get him out the British had to send an army from India. This force, 32,000 strong, duly marched from Massawa to Magdala, building its own rail-

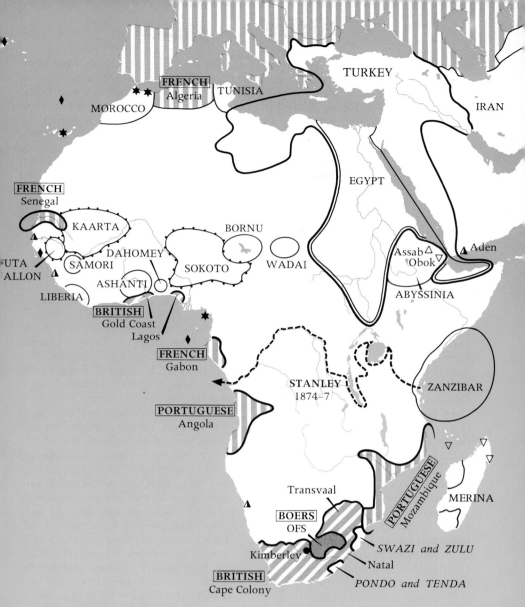

TURKEY

IRAN

FRENCH
Algeria

TUNISIA

MOROCCO

EGYPT

FRENCH
Senegal

KAARTA

BORNU

Assab
Obok

Aden

'UTA
ALLON

DAHOMEY

SAMORI

SOKOTO

WADAI

ABYSSINIA

ASHANTI

LIBERIA

BRITISH
Gold Coast
Lagos

FRENCH
Gabon

STANLEY
1874–7

ZANZIBAR

PORTUGUESE
Angola

Transvaal

BOERS
OFS

Kimberley

PORTUGUESE
Mozambique

MERINA

SWAZI and ZULU

Natal

BRITISH
Cape Colony

PONDO and TENDA

Islands and enclaves
◆ Portuguese
✶ Spanish
▲ British
▽ French
△ Italian

AD **1878**

way as it went, released the Consul (who was found to be in good working order), and then returned to the coast and sailed back to India. It left behind it an Abyssinia rapidly relapsing into anarchy: Theodore, who had shot himself when Magdala fell, appeared to have laboured in vain.

This was not so. A new Abyssinian king, John IV, followed Theodore's example and managed to make his rule effective through most of the country. His forces proved strong enough to repel the Egyptian invasions of 1874–5 and thereafter he was able to take advantage of the subsequent recoil of the Egyptian empire to expand Abyssinia's frontiers beyond their traditional limits.

There is not much to report on the other African kingdoms during this period: al-Hajj Umar of Kaarta conquered Masina in 1862; a Mande *condottiere* named Samori Toure set up a principality at Bisandugu in present-day Guinea in 1866; the British on the Gold Coast marched into Kumasi, the capital of the Ashanti kingdom, in 1874 but then marched out again. There is, however, a very important change in the way the map is drawn because the shadings used till now to show the distribution of the various sub-Saharan peoples have been dropped. And so have the names of all but the most important native kingdoms. From now on if you want to place a tribe like the Masai either geographically or ethnically, you will have to turn back to earlier maps – or use the index.

This change – this over-simplification – is necessary if the increasingly complicated events of the next hundred years are to be presented legibly. But it is also symbolic of a change in the real world: the temporary demotion of the African to a secondary role in African history. For we are now nearing the beginning of the 'scramble for Africa', the period when the colonial powers moved in on the continent and divided it up between them. For the next seventy odd years, which means the next half dozen maps, it is the Europeans who dominate the scene: the Africans are barely visible.

Why did the Europeans suddenly move into a continent that they had been hanging around the edge of for the previous five centuries? A large part of the answer lies in the contemporary music hall song which gave the word jingo to the language:

We don't want to fight, but, by jingo if we do,
We've got the ships, we've got the men,
    we've got the money too.

There was a mood of unbounded confidence in Europe, and it wasn't misplaced: no power in the Old World could hope to resist European arms; immense and ancient empires like China's could be slapped down by the deployment of trivial numbers of men. And the financial resources were there to sustain longer campaigns if necessary. Unlike Egypt, Europe generated enough wealth to fight unprofitable wars.

In Africa the technological advantage of the Europeans had been apparent for a long time: what had prevented Britain creating an African empire to match its empire in India was the dreadful mortality caused among Europeans by African diseases. The discovery that a daily dose of quinine would protect against the most deadly of these, sub-tertian malaria, was made as early as 1847 by a British naval surgeon: in 1854 a twelve-man team sailed up the Niger and Benue and back without loss, an unheard-of thing for a generation of seamen that had been brought up on the rhyme:

Beware, beware the Bight of Benin
For few come out, though many go in.

Now even the deadliest part of Africa lay open to European exploitation. One of the first consequences of this was the British acquisition of Lagos in 1861.

Of course a money incentive was needed to get things really moving. The most dramatic one was the discovery of diamonds at Kimberley on the border between the Cape Colony and the Orange Free State in 1867. Immediately there was a rush of British immigrants, an influx of British capital, and, following the annexation of Kimberley by the Cape Colony in 1873, the creation of a British power base in South Africa that was capable of exerting its own pressure on events. At the opposite end of the continent the opening of the Suez Canal attracted European investment to the barren coast of the Red Sea, for the new steamships needed coaling stations: the British already had one in Aden (established in 1839); the French set up theirs at Obok in 1862, the Italians bought a site at Assab in 1869.

As the world's leading sea power the British were pretty well bound to become the world's leading imperialists. Running them a close second were the French. This doesn't reflect the political pecking order in Europe, where Germany had soundly beaten the French in 1870 and so become the undoubted number one, but Germany was not (as yet) a sea power and Bismarck, the chancellor who had masterminded Germany's rise to this position, pooh-poohed any idea of a German overseas empire. In fact, for historic reasons, third place was held by a power that was completely negligible in current European terms, Portugal. And fourth place was to go to an individual, King Leopold of Belgium.

Leopold's story is an interesting one. As his parliament had made it clear that it wasn't interested in colonial adventures, he was forced to use his own money to back his ideas. His original plan was to set up some sort of trading network in Cameroon: then in 1878 he met Stanley. Although Stanley was keen to see the Zaire basin opened up commercially he was looking to the British to do this. It took the combination of British apathy and Leopold's charm to persuade Stanley that he ought to accept the Belgian king's backing.

The practical beginnings of Leopold's colonial venture – and indeed of the European empire-building period generally – belong to the next map, not this one. However, one or two encroachments are already visible: the French are a bit further up the Senegal, have a new station in present-day Guinea (then called Rivières du Sud) and, thanks largely to the initiative of the explorer-administrator de Brazza, are better established in Gabon. The British have advanced their frontier in the Cape, not only to take in Kimberley but also more of the east coast (1866), most of Basutoland (1871: the rest had been annexed by the Orange Free State Boers in 1866) and all of the Transvaal (1876).

The Boers of the Transvaal were, for the moment, letting the British take them over because their own government had been bankrupted by wars with the local Bantu. To please the Boers the British decided to break the Zulu *impis* once and for all and in 1879 they marched into Zululand. In the first battle at Isandhlwana, the British ran out of ammunition and got slaughtered, but three months later they were back, this time with machine guns. The introduction of this new weapon, whose fire power was enough to compensate for the most Blimpish blunder, marks the real beginning of the new era. To quote one more rhyme, all that a British officer now needed to remember was contained in Belloc's unheroic couplet:

Whatever happens we have got
The Maxim gun and they have not.

THE 'scramble for Africa' is no misnomer: during the 1880s the continent was carved up so fast that by the end of the decade the outlines of the various empires were pretty well decided. This map shows the halfway stage when the allocation of the coastline was all but complete but the division of the interior had barely begun.

There are various ways of looking at the 'scramble'. Chronologically it is fair to say that the French started it. Probably as a reaction to their defeat in Europe the French began to behave aggressively all around the globe including, in Africa, Tunisia (made into a protectorate in 1881), Senegal (where there was a steady advance to the Niger over the years 1879–83) and Gabon (where de Brazza brought the Fang peoples of the interior into dependence in 1879–82). But diplomatically it was undoubtedly the British that upset the status quo. In 1881 a Colonel Arabi led a nationalist revolt in Egypt, hardly a surprising development in a country that was being run by foreigners, but one that immediately caused the European debt-holders to start lobbying their governments. The British intervened 'to restore order', one thing led to another and by 1882 they found themselves in accidental and – so they assured everyone – temporary occupation of the country. The French, who had been unable to muster sufficient force sufficiently quickly to join in, were furious. Egypt had been an international protectorate with France playing the predominant role among the supervising powers: now it had suddenly become, *de facto* if not *de jure*, part of the British empire. It was an outrage.

It was also an excuse. If Britain could help itself to bits of Africa so could everyone else. Indeed national dignity positively required that they do so. Even Bismark gave way to the clamour: in 1884 he proclaimed protectorates over the areas where German missionaries were active – Togo, Cameroon and South-West Africa. He also announced a vaguely defined suzerainty over the sultanate of Zanzibar, its hinterland and its offshoot the sultanate of Witu (W on the map). This overlapped established British interests and so to sort out what belonged to whom here and in other parts of Africa all the interested parties were invited to attend a special conference in Berlin at the end of the year. The result was the colonial carve-up shown opposite.

The map also shows two important developments in the interior. In the upper Nile the Egyptians have been thrown out by the Sudanese under the leadership of their *mahdi*, Mohamed Ahmed. Starting in 1881 the *mahdi's* forces conquered everything previously held by the Egyptians south of the second cataract except the Red Sea littoral (which was taken over by the British and Italians) and the province of Equatoria (which continued to function in complete isolation from the rest of the world under its last governor, the German Emin Pasha). Meanwhile the other major river basin in Central Africa, the basin of the Zaire (Congo), was being re-explored by Stanley, now acting as agent for Leopold of the Belgians. Between 1879 and 1884 Stanley set up a chain of trading stations along the river: the result of this investment was a personal empire for Leopold (recognized as such at the Berlin Conference) which, if it funnelled down to the width of the river at its Atlantic end, expanded to cover a potentially enormous area in the centre of the continent.

Note that the Transvaal Boers have thrown out the British and re-established their independence (1881).

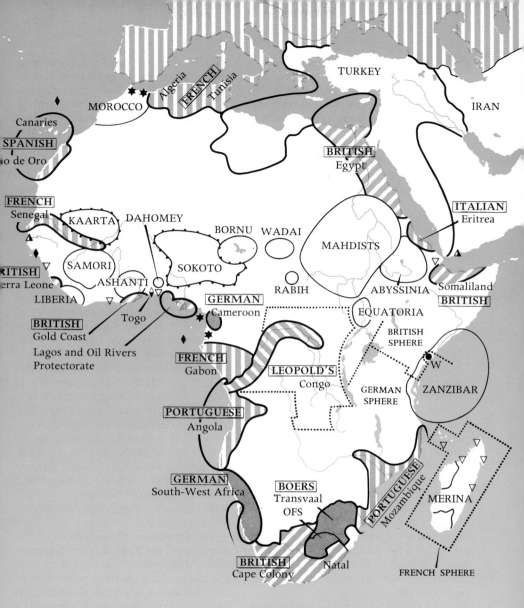

Islands and enclaves
- ◆ Portuguese
- ✦ Spanish
- ◊ German
- △ British
- ▽ French
- W Witu

AD **1885**

THE British were somewhat taken aback by the reaction of the other powers to their occupation of Egypt, and at the Berlin Conference, when everyone else was putting forward more and more extravagant claims, they did little more than defend their existing positions. However it wasn't long before they recovered their balance and in the later 1880s they showed that when it came to empire-building they didn't need to take lessons from anyone. Britain's come-back was the easier because it soon became clear that the Germans weren't really interested in Africa: they agreed to transfer their protectorates over Witu and Zanzibar to Britain in 1890 and they accepted a northern limit to their East African sphere that gave the British Uganda. All this in return for Heligoland, a tiny island off the German coast which the British had been using as a naval base since the Napoleonic wars.

The British aim in East Africa was to prevent any other European power reaching the Upper Nile. They were persuaded that this was necessary by Sir Samuel Baker, who assured the government of the day (and the readers of *The Times*) that such a power, using modern engineering methods, could easily divert the waters of the White Nile, so bringing desolation to Egypt and disaster to the British empire. The best that can be said for this idea is that it gave British policy in this part of Africa a consistency which maybe contributed to its success.

South-Central Africa also came under British control at this time. The driving force here was Cecil Rhodes, an English-born financial wizard who had made himself a multi-millionaire by cornering South Africa's diamond output and was prepared to use his millions to expand Britain's African empire. His agents travelled north along the routes opened up by Livingstone a generation earlier, signing treaties of protection with the Tswana (a Sotho people: the spelling favoured at this time was Bechuana, hence Bechuanaland), the Ndebele (Matabeleland), the Shona (Mashonaland) and, beyond the Zambesi, nearly all the tribes between the upper reaches of the river and Lake Nyasa. By 1890, when he became Prime Minister of the Cape Colony, Rhodes had put paid forever to Portuguese dreams of linking Angola and Mozambique, as well as depriving the Boer states of any hope of expanding to west or north.

In West Africa Britain did little on the ground, though her diplomats saw to it that France and Germany respected her sphere of interest in Nigeria. By contrast the French were very active: they annexed Futa Jallon in 1888 and kept up a constant pressure on the two most important potentates of the upper Niger, Sheikh Ahmadu of Kaarta, son and heir of al-Hajj Umar, and Samori Toure, the Mande conqueror who had brought most of the Guinea highlands under his control in the 1870s. The French were obviously intending to move further along the Niger as soon as they could solve the logistics of the operation. They were the only serious rivals the British had in Africa.

Not serious at all, except to themselves, were the Italians. They had completed their conquest of Eritrea by now and the British gave them permission to take over Zanzibar's stake in Somaliland. This gave them ideas about putting the squeeze on Abyssinia, which was in a poor way again – King John had just been killed fighting the Mahdists – and they actually got the new Abyssinian king, Menelik, to sign a treaty recognizing Italy's 'special interest' in his country.

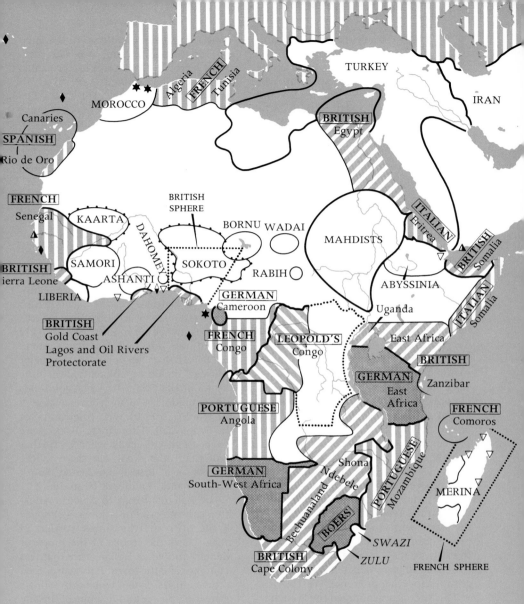

TURKEY

IRAN

FRENCH
Algeria
Tunisia

MOROCCO

Canaries

SPANISH
Rio de Oro

BRITISH
Egypt

FRENCH
Senegal

KAARTA

DAHOMEY

BORNU WADAI

BRITISH
SPHERE

MAHDISTS

ITALIAN
Eritrea

BRITISH
Somalia

BRITISH
ierra Leone

SAMORI

ASHANTI

LIBERIA

SOKOTO

RABIH

ABYSSINIA

ITALIAN
Somalia

BRITISH
Gold Coast
Lagos and Oil Rivers
Protectorate

GERMAN
Cameroon

Uganda

East Africa

BRITISH
Zanzibar

FRENCH
Congo

LEOPOLD'S
Congo

GERMAN
East
Africa

FRENCH
Comoros

PORTUGUESE
Angola

GERMAN
South-West Africa

Shona

Ndebele

MERINA

Bechuanaland

PORTUGUESE
Mozambique

BOERS

SWAZI

ZULU

BRITISH
Cape Colony

FRENCH SPHERE

Islands and enclaves

♦ Portuguese
★ Spanish
⬧ German
▲ British
▽ French

AD 1890

IN 1896–8 the British attacked and destroyed the Mahdist state in the Sudan. As they pushed up the White Nile they found a French expedition that had crossed over from the Congo and planted the tricolour slap in the middle of the British sphere (at Kodok, known then as Fashoda): it was ordered off, much to the chagrin of the French, who seriously considered going to war over the incident. The British remained firm, and they were firm with Leopold too. The previous year an expedition of his had driven the Mahdists from Lado (modern Rejaf) in Equatoria: this was also within the British sphere and Leopold was told that although he could keep this enclave during his lifetime it must be returned to Sudanese (meaning British) control on his death. A peripheral Sudanese province, Darfur, they were prepared to leave to a sultan of the old royal line.

The French didn't really have much reason to be sore about the Nile; they were having things pretty much their own way in West Africa. They eliminated Ahmadu of Kaarta in 1893 (after which Joffre, the future victor of the Marne, was able to enter Timbuctoo) and the more resilient Samori in 1898. Firmly established on the middle Niger, they proceeded to link this new territory – the French Sudan – with their positions on the Ivory Coast and, further to the east, with the newly established province of Dahomey (conquered 1894). In this way they created a solid block of sub-Saharan provinces that in 1895 were grouped together as French West Africa.

This success encouraged the French to try an even more ambitious link-up. In 1900 three columns converged on Lake Chad: one from Algeria, one from French West Africa and one from the French Congo. The Lake Chad region, the ancient kingdom of Bornu, was currently being terrorized by a slave raider named Rabih who had moved there from his original haunts south of Darfur. The French columns managed to rendezvous successfully, dispose of Rabih and so establish a connection, tenuous but tangible, between French North Africa, French West Africa and the French Congo.

In South Africa Cecil Rhodes had Rhodesia named after him (1895). This may have gone to his head, because he then overreached himself badly by attempting a coup against the Boers (the Jameson raid of 1896). The British government had to intervene and even then the war opened with some humiliating defeats for the local British forces (1899). The arrival of major units of the British army in early 1900 quickly turned the tide and by that summer the British had occupied all the major centres, including Bloemfontein (the capital of the OFS), the Rand goldfields (discovered in 1856 and the real cause of the trouble) and Pretoria (the capital of the Transvaal). Though the Boers were to wage a bitter guerilla war for a further two years the final outcome of the conflict – a British-dominated South Africa – could no longer be in doubt.

The Italian attempt to squeeze Abyssinia came to grief at Adowa, just south of the Eritrean–Abyssinian border, in 1896. There the troops of the Emperor Menelik routed an Italian army that was trying to take the town: Italy was forced to give up its claims to be Abyssinia's protecting power and its hope of linking Eritrea with Somaliland. The French conquered most of Madagascar (starting 1895): they had earlier annexed the Comoros (1886).

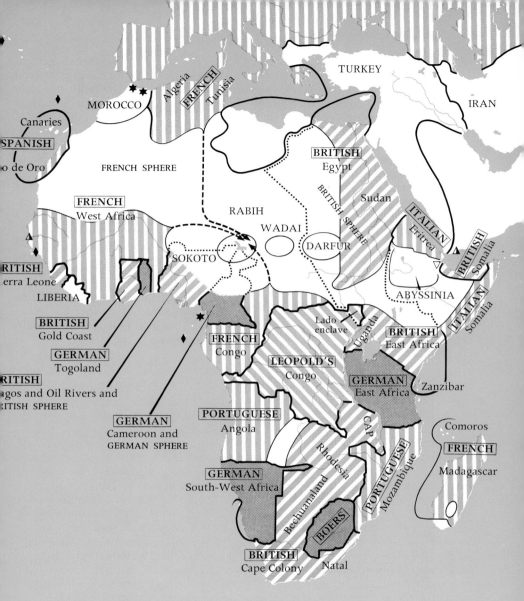

TURKEY

IRAN

MOROCCO

Algeria

FRENCH

Tunisia

Canaries

SPANISH

o de Oro

FRENCH SPHERE

BRITISH

Egypt

Sudan

BRITISH SPHERE

ITALIAN

Eritrea

BRITISH

Somalia

FRENCH
West Africa

RABIH

WADAI

DARFUR

RITISH
erra Leone

LIBERIA

SOKOTO

ABYSSINIA

ITALIAN
Somalia

BRITISH
Gold Coast

Lado
enclave

Uganda

BRITISH
East Africa

GERMAN
Togoland

FRENCH
Congo

LEOPOLD'S
Congo

GERMAN
East Africa

Zanzibar

RITISH
agos and Oil Rivers and
RITISH SPHERE

Comoros

FRENCH

Madagascar

GERMAN
Cameroon and
GERMAN SPHERE

PORTUGUESE
Angola

CAP

GERMAN
South-West Africa

Rhodesia

PORTUGUESE
Mozambique

Bechuanaland

GERMAN
South-West Africa

BOERS

BRITISH
Cape Colony

Natal

Islands and enclaves

♦ Portuguese
✴ Spanish
△ British
▽ French
CAP = Central African Protectorate (**BRITISH**)

AD **1900**

THE period between the ending of the Boer War (in 1902) and the outbreak of the First World War (in 1914) was one of consolidation for the European empires. The French and British very nearly completed their occupation of their respective spheres and most of the frontiers between them and the other colonial administrations now received their definitive form. Enlivening this somewhat dull process were a couple of crises (in 1905–6 and 1911) over who was going to get Morocco. Eventually it was divided between France (90 per cent) and Spain (10 per cent), with Germany being compensated by the transfer to Cameroon of some of French Equatorial Africa (an agglomeration formed in 1910 by the addition of the new Chad colony to the existing French Congo).

The main events in the British sphere were the conquest of northern Nigeria in 1901–3, the closing of the gap between the Sudan and Uganda (with the Lado enclave coming in on Leopold's death in 1909), and the formation of the Union of South Africa by the merger of the Cape Colony, Natal, the Orange Free State and the Transvaal (1910). The white population of South Africa was now above the 1.25 million mark, comfortably ahead of the figure for white settlers in Algeria, which was 0.75 million. It was also a larger proportion of the total population, 22 per cent of 6 million as opposed to 14 per cent of 5.25 million. These two remained the only white populations of significant size in the continent.

The Italians took coastal Tripolitania and Cyrenaica from the Turks in 1911–12 but didn't succeed in establishing themselves in the interior.

SPANISH
Morocco

FRENCH
Morocco

Algeria

FRENCH
Tunisia

Tripoli

ITALIAN
Cyrenaica

TURKEY

IRAN

Canaries

PANISH

io de Oro

Egypt

BRITISH

Sudan

FRENCH
West Africa

ITALIAN
Eritrea

BRITISH
Somalia

Darfur

BRITISH
ra Leone

LIBERIA

BRITISH
Nigeria

ABYSSINIA

ITALIAN
Somalia

GERMAN
Cameroon

Equatorial Africa

BRITISH
Gold Coast

GERMAN
Togoland

FRENCH

BELGIAN
Congo

Uganda

BRITISH
East Africa

GERMAN
East Africa

Zanzibar

PORTUGUESE
Angola

Nyasa-
land

Comoros

FRENCH
Madagascar

Rhodesia

PORTUGUESE
Mozambique

GERMAN
South-West Africa

Bechuanaland

BRITISH
Union of South Africa

Islands and enclaves

♦ Portuguese
✶ Spanish
△ British
▽ French

AD **1914**

IN 1914 the German army invaded Belgium, precipitating the First World War. Four years later, exhausted by a contest that seemed as far as ever from military solution, the German people threw in the towel, threw out the Kaiser and gave up – for the time being, anyway – their ideas of ruling the world. The victors had many wounds to lick and few spoils to divide: Germany's overseas empire, about the only asset that could be put on the chopping block right away, was quickly disposed of.

Britain and France had put more into the war than any of the other Allies and there was never any doubt about their getting the lion's share of the German colonies in Africa. Britain took South-West Africa and German East Africa (bar Rwanda and Burundi, which went to Belgium), France took Cameroon (except for a strip on the west which was attached to British Nigeria), Togoland they divided between them. All of these territories were technically allocated by the 'League of Nations', the inter-war prototype of the United Nations, but there wasn't much practical difference between them and straightforward colonies.

The Turks fought on the German side in the First World War: among those who responded to their call for a *jihad* against the Allied powers was the sultan of Darfur, who got himself killed and his country annexed to the Sudan as a result (1916). The *jihad* waged against the Italians (who were on the Allied side this time) by the bedouin of the interior of Libya was far more successful: under the leadership of the Sanusi brotherhood the Arabs kept the Italians huddled up in a few seaports for the duration. When the war was over the Italians were compensated for this discomfort by the transfer of Kenya's north-eastern province to Italian Somaliland (a very reasonable move as the population was entirely Somali) and some rectifications to the frontier of Libya at French and British expense. Actually occupying the interior of Libya was something the Italians found more difficult than redrawing its frontiers: Sanusi resistance in the hinterland of Cyrenaica wasn't finally overcome till 1928.

The 1912 treaty by which the powers agreed to the division of Morocco between France and Spain contained a clause internationalizing Tangier: when the First World War broke out Spain withdrew her assent to this but the Tangier international zone was finally set up in 1924.

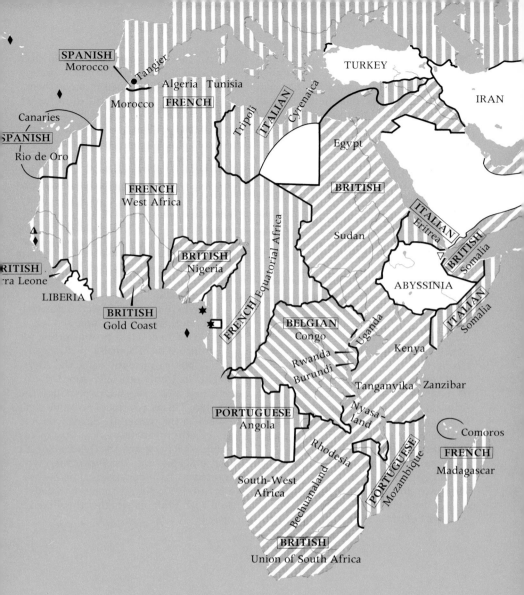

SPANISH
Morocco

Tangier

Algeria Tunisia

Morocco FRENCH

TURKEY

IRAN

Canaries

SPANISH
Rio de Oro

Tripoli ITALIAN Cyrenaica

Egypt

BRITISH

ITALIAN
Eritrea

FRENCH
West Africa

BRITISH
Sierra Leone

BRITISH
Nigeria

FRENCH Equatorial Africa

Sudan

BRITISH
Somalia

LIBERIA

BRITISH
Gold Coast

BELGIAN
Congo

Uganda

ABYSSINIA

ITALIAN
Somalia

Rwanda
Burundi

Kenya

Tanganyika Zanzibar

PORTUGUESE
Angola

Nyasa-
land

Comoros

Rhodesia

PORTUGUESE
Mozambique

FRENCH
Madagascar

South-West
Africa

Bechuanaland

BRITISH
Union of South Africa

Islands and enclaves
♦ Portuguese
✳ Spanish
△ British
▽ French

AD **1925**

IN 1935 the Italians invaded Abyssinia again. Mussolini, the Italian dictator who invented fascism, was determined to wipe out the memory of Adowa and this time things were done better – better, that is, if you count the use of mustard gas as an improvement. By May 1936 Abyssinian resistance was broken. Four years later, after the Germans had got the Second World War started, the Italians briefly achieved their goal of occupying the entire Horn by forcing the British out of their part of Somaliland.

Retribution was not long in coming. The British returned in 1941 and soon overcame Italy's East African forces. They also – despite the intervention of the German Afrika corps – drove the Italians from Libya (1943). When the war came to an end in 1945 the British position in Africa had never seemed stronger.

Of course it wasn't really. An upsurge of nationalist sentiment was making Britain's imperial role impossible in two key areas: India and Egypt. In 1947 the British recognized this: they agreed, with surprisingly good humour, to leave India and, much more grudgingly, to get out of Egypt bar the Suez Canal. Not that there was any point hanging on to the canal once India was gone, but out of some sort of obsolete strategic reflex the British insisted on it: in doing so they lost what little goodwill the evacuation of the rest of Egypt had brought them.

Another area where British influence was waning was South Africa. In the 1948 elections the Nationalist (Boer) Party managed to win a majority of the seats (though not of the votes) and was able to begin the institution of its policy of apartheid. The essence of this was the exclusion of the black majority from any share in political or economic power – forever. On the map this Boer revival is indicated by the use of solid tinting over the area of Union government: the two enclaves still controlled by the British Colonial Office, Swaziland and Basutoland, are banded as before.

Elsewhere the British were preparing Libya and Somalia for independence. They tried to create a better outline for the future state of Somalia by asking the Ethiopians – to use the name the Abyssinians had now officially adopted – to cede to it their easternmost province, the Ogaden. This is a desert of no value at all except to the scattered Somali who live in it. Unfortunately the Ethiopians wouldn't have it and the Ogaden Somali lost out. So did the Eritreans, who wanted to be independent but eventually (in 1952) found themselves federated with Ethiopia whether they liked it or not.

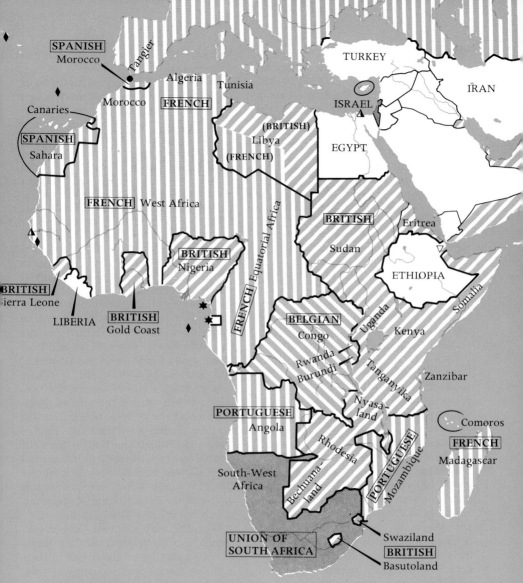

SPANISH
Morocco

Tangier

Algeria

Tunisia

FRENCH

Morocco

TURKEY

IRAN

ISRAEL

Canaries

SPANISH
Sahara

(BRITISH)
Libya
(FRENCH)

EGYPT

FRENCH West Africa

BRITISH

Eritrea

FRENCH Equatorial Africa

BRITISH
Nigeria

BRITISH
Sudan

ETHIOPIA

Somalia

BRITISH
Sierra Leone

LIBERIA

BRITISH
Gold Coast

BELGIAN
Congo

Uganda

Kenya

Rwanda
Burundi

Tanganyika

Zanzibar

PORTUGUESE
Angola

Nyasa-
land

Rhodesia

Comoros

FRENCH
Madagascar

PORTUGUESE Mozambique

South-West
Africa

Bechuana-
land

Swaziland

**UNION OF
SOUTH AFRICA**

BRITISH
Basutoland

Islands and enclaves
♦ Portuguese
✶ Spanish
△ British
▽ French

AD **1950**

DURING the 1950s the process of decolonization gathered speed. The British left Libya in 1951 and the Sudan and the Suez Canal base in 1956. That same year the French withdrew from Tunisia and they and the Spanish from Morocco. Much less happy was the situation in Algeria, where the million-strong white settler community was insisting that the French government implement its quite unrealistic promise to integrate Algeria with France: by 1954 there was a major war in progress here. In this struggle the French army usually came out on top in the settled areas, in the daytime and in the daily communiqués, while the F L N, the Algerian Liberation Front, gradually won over the hinterland, the Moslem majority and the sympathies of the international community.

A more dramatic, if less important, bit of back-pedalling by the colonial powers came towards the end of 1956. As a by-product of events that were actually peripheral to African interests – American support of Israel, the Cold War between America and Russia – Egypt and America fell out. The Americans cut off their aid: Egypt responded by nationalizing the Suez Canal Company whose 100-year concession still had thirteen years to run. This didn't mean anything to the Americans, who hadn't any shares in the Company, but infuriated the British and French, who had: they persuaded the Israelis to launch a *blitzkrieg* against Egypt, so giving them the excuse to intervene and – shades of 1881 – 'restore order'. The operation was so immediately and decisively condemned by world opinion that it had to be abandoned before it was properly begun. Clearly imperialism – or

at least imperialism of the old gunboat sort – was dead.

Black Africa had been expected by all concerned to have to wait much longer than the Arab north for its freedom. However, the wind of change was now blowing away the old empires so fast that there were as many sovereign states as colonies south of the Sahara by 1960. The first two to achieve independence were the Gold Coast (which took the name Ghana) in 1957 and French Guinea (which called itself Guinea) in 1958. In 1960 came the grand slam. Britain conferred independence on the giant among African states, Nigeria: France got out of Black Africa entirely, recognizing as individual countries each of the administrative units that had formed the conglomerates of French West Africa (Mauritania, the French Sudan – under the name Mali – Niger, Senegal, Upper Volta, Ivory Coast, Togo and Dahomey) and French Equatorial Africa (Chad, Ubangi-Shari – which became the Central African Republic – Cameroon, Gabon and the Congo). In addition the Belgians withdrew from the Belgian Congo, the British and Italians from the two halves of Somaliland (the Italians had been allowed back to their half by the United Nations to help prepare for this day) and the French from Madagascar, which became the Malagasy Republic.

Note the way the two Congos (ex-French and ex-Belgian) identify themselves by tacking on the names of their capitals. Also, Egypt's change of title: the country's last king, the fat and foolish Farouk, was expelled after a revolt by army officers (1952); the republic they proclaimed then was merged with Syria in 1958 to form the United Arab Republic.

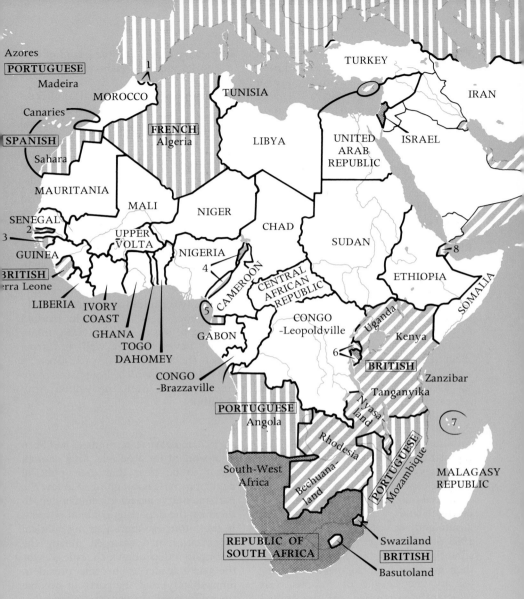

Azores
PORTUGUESE
Madeira

Canaries

SPANISH

Sahara

MAURITANIA

SENEGAL
2
3
GUINEA

BRITISH
rra Leone

LIBERIA

MOROCCO

MALI

UPPER
VOLTA

IVORY
COAST
GHANA
TOGO
DAHOMEY

NIGER

NIGERIA

4

5

GABON

CONGO
-Brazzaville

TUNISIA

FRENCH
Algeria

LIBYA

CHAD

CAMEROON

CENTRAL
AFRICAN
REPUBLIC

CONGO
-Leopoldville

TURKEY

UNITED
ARAB
REPUBLIC

SUDAN

Uganda

6

BRITISH

Tanganyika

IRAN

ISRAEL

ETHIOPIA

SOMALIA

Kenya

Zanzibar

8

PORTUGUESE
Angola

South-West
Africa

Bechuana-
land

Nyasa-
land

Rhodesia

7

PORTUGUESE
Mozambique

MALAGASY
REPUBLIC

**REPUBLIC OF
SOUTH AFRICA**

Swaziland
BRITISH
Basutoland

Colonial islands and enclaves
1 **SPANISH**   Ceuta and Melilla
2 **BRITISH**   Gambia
3 **PORTUGUESE** Cape Verde Islands and Guinea
4 **BRITISH**   Cameroon
5 **SPANISH**   Fernando Po and Rio Muni
6 **BELGIAN**   Rwanda and Burundi
7 **FRENCH**   Comoros
8 **FRENCH**   Somaliland

AD **1960**

THE process of decolonization continued relatively smoothly in the early 1960s with the British withdrawing from Sierra Leone, Tanganyika and their strip of Cameroon in 1961 (the people in the northern half of the strip voted to join Nigeria, those in the south to join the state of Cameroon), Uganda in 1962, Kenya and Zanzibar in 1963, Zambia (ex-Northern Rhodesia) and Malawi (ex-Nyasaland) in 1964 and the Gambia in 1965. At this point things started to go wrong. There were 250,000 British settlers in Rhodesia (ex-Southern Rhodesia) and that was just enough to run a South African style white supremacist state. In 1965 these Rhodesian settlers declared themselves the independent government of the country and its six million African inhabitants. The British refused to consider using force against the rebels, the attempt to bring them to heel by economic sanctions was a flop, and, temporarily at least, Rhodesia succeeded in joining the South African bloc.

Besides South Africa and Rhodesia this bloc consisted of Angola and Mozambique, which the Portuguese declared they would never leave. Minor blemishes on it were the three enclaves on which the British Colonial Office now conferred independence – Botswana (ex-Bechuanaland) and Lesotho (ex-Basutoland) in 1966 and Swaziland in 1968. South-West Africa continued to be administered by the South Africans: their mandate to do so, originally granted by the League of Nations, was reluctantly confirmed by the United Nations in 1966.

Outside southern Africa independence was now the rule. The French finally gave up in Algeria (in 1962, after eight years of war), the Belgians left Rwanda and Burundi (also 1962), the Spanish returned Ifni to Morocco (1969) and created the new state of Equatorial Guinea by combining the island of Fernando Po with the mainland colony of Rio Muni (1968).

A number of Africa's royal families re-emerged in the immediate post-colonial period. One that did well was the royal house of Morocco, which is still in power today (meaning mid-1978): one that did badly was the Arab sultanate of Zanzibar; only two weeks after independence the sultan was thrown out by a revolutionary group representing the islands' black majority. This new government immediately made an offer of union to Tanganyika which was quickly accepted and consummated. Tanzania – the name adopted by the combination – has been a political success: its two halves have grown steadily closer ever since. This is in marked contrast to the Egyptian–Syrian union, which never worked well and from which the Syrians finally withdrew in 1961 (despite which Egypt has continued to call itself the United Arab Republic).

*

By 1970 most African countries had been independent for a decade, long enough for it to be clear that their political development was not going to follow the parliamentary model recommended to them by the departing colonial powers. In the countries where a strong political organization had emerged during the run-up to independence the rule was for the party leader to become president (immediately) and the party to become the only one in the country (after a few years). This was the case for example in Ghana, where Kwame Nkrumah had established the Convention People's Party in a dominating position well before independence. Alternatively when the politicians failed to establish an effective government the military stepped in and did it for them: the

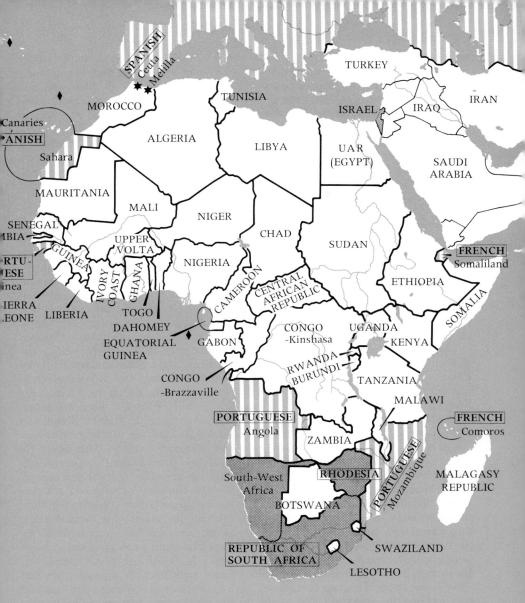

SPANISH Ceuta Melilla

★ ★

TURKEY

IRAN

ISRAEL IRAQ

MOROCCO

TUNISIA

Canaries
ÁNISH

Sahara

ALGERIA

LIBYA

UAR
(EGYPT)

SAUDI
ARABIA

MAURITANIA

MALI

NIGER

CHAD

SUDAN

FRENCH
Somaliland

SENEGAL
MBIA

RTU-
ESE
inea

GUINEA

UPPER
VOLTA

NIGERIA

CAMEROON

CENTRAL
AFRICAN
REPUBLIC

ETHIOPIA

SOMALIA

IERRA
EONE

LIBERIA

IVORY
COAST

GHANA

TOGO

DAHOMEY

EQUATORIAL
GUINEA

GABON

CONGO
-Kinshasa

UGANDA

KENYA

CONGO
-Brazzaville

RWANDA
BURUNDI

TANZANIA

MALAWI

FRENCH
Comoros

PORTUGUESE
Angola

ZAMBIA

PORTUGUESE
Mozambique

MALAGASY
REPUBLIC

South-West
Africa

RHODESIA

BOTSWANA

REPUBLIC OF
SOUTH AFRICA

SWAZILAND

LESOTHO

◆ Portuguese islands
★ Spanish enclaves

AD 1970

textbook case here is the Belgian Congo, where the Belgians left before anyone expected them to and there was near anarchy until General Mobutu took over in 1965. Not that Mobutu's government hasn't had its troubles, but it has survived to the present day (again meaning mid-1978). Civilian figures of comparable longevity include Habib Bourguiba of Tunisia, Leopold Senghor of Senegal, Sékou Touré of Guinea-Conakry, Felix Houphouet-Boigny of the Ivory Coast, Ahmadou Ahidjo of Cameroon and a remarkable group of founding fathers in East Africa − Jomo Kenyatta of Kenya, Julius Nyerere of Tanzania, Kenneth Kaunda of Zambia and Hastings Banda of Malawi. All these men came to power on independence day and have now ruled so long that it has become difficult to imagine their countries without them.

The military men are a much more uneven lot. At one end of the scale is Colonel Nasser, the man who masterminded the officers' coup that expelled King Farouk from Egypt in 1952 and the unchallenged ruler of the country from 1954 until his death in 1970. Though Nasser's government was always autocratic, and in its later days became oppressively so, no one has questioned his dedication to the welfare of his people nor his initial success in improving the quality of life for the ordinary Egyptian. To the world at large − and to the Arab nations in particular − his finest hour was undoubtedly his stand against the British−French−Israeli onslaught of 1956: it was an act of courage that earned him international standing. But in the long run this status proved a dubious asset: radical movements everywhere badgered Egypt for support and the result was a diversion abroad of energies and resources that were desperately needed at home. In 1967 a new war with Israel saw the Egyptian army routed in six days and demonstrated how wide a

gap there was between Nasser's estimate of Egypt's strength and the nation's actual capacity. His lieutenant and successor Anwar Sadat inevitably presented a lower profile: it was probably to Egypt's advantage that he did so.

By the time Nasser died military governments similar to his were running most of North Africa: they seemed to have the right style for Arab countries trying to find their place in the world. In Algeria the austere Colonel Boumedienne had displaced Ben Bella, leader of the political wing of the F L N, back in 1965, but the vintage year for army coups was 1969: within a matter of months officers took over the reins of government in Libya, Somalia and − not for the first time − Sudan. Libya's Colonel Gaddafy, who ousted the Sanusi king installed by the British eighteen years earlier, dedicated himself to re-establishing the purity and international status of Islam. He had massive oil revenues with which to finance his *jihad*, but religious fundamentalism seemed even to his Arab neighbours an inadequate answer to the problems of the twentieth century: both Egypt (in 1973) and Tunisia (in 1974) eventually rejected his offers of political union. General Numeiry's task − and achievement − was to hold his country together. Like all the states that straddled the Sahel, the Sudan has a built-in tendency to polarize into an Arab-oriented north and a Black African south: when Numeiry took over, this antagonism had long since escalated into open war and the southerners seemed determined to fight their way to complete independence of Khartoum. His grant of autonomy to the Southern Region was the stroke of statesmanship the situation needed: it put an end to the civil war and instituted a surprisingly successful national reconciliation.

In Black Africa the military men were

a good deal less impressive than this, and a lot less impressive than their civilian counterparts: none of them achieved the stature of a Kenyatta, Nyerere, Kaunda or Banda. Perhaps because of this the idea of civilian government has not lost its appeal here in the same way it has in the north of the continent. When Kwame Nkrumah of Ghana was ousted by the army in 1966 the military leaders insisted that their government was provisional and that power would be handed back to the civilians when the economic disasters caused by Nkrumah's extravagance had been repaired. And to everyone's surprise the generals did in fact step down in 1969.

Nigeria is another country where the generals took over the government (in 1966) but promised to hand it back to the civilians when they had restored order. They haven't done so yet (the promise is for 1979), but then Nigeria has had its problems, notably a civil war in 1967–70. This was caused by the Ibo's attempt to secede: the state they set up – they called it Biafra – received diplomatic recognition from several African countries and was extinguished only after bitter fighting. Since then the Federal Military Government has divided Nigeria into smaller, more evenly sized units, which should make it more difficult for the same sort of thing to happen again.

Considering that Africa's frontiers were drawn by the colonial powers to suit themselves it is not surprising that some of the newly independent states had a difficult task holding themselves together. Most of the new countries were far bigger than the tribal units to which the Black African gives his fiercest loyalty and some of them are composed – like Sudan and Nigeria – of peoples who are in ethnic, religious and historical opposition to each other. The remarkable thing is that so far none of the secessionist movements has succeeded, not even in Zaire (Congo-Kinshasa), which is vast, was abandoned by the Belgians without any administrative preparation and as a result had a peculiarly unsteady beginning. To keep Zaire together has meant calling in European troops from time to time which, though unwelcome to other Africans and undignified in itself, has at least enabled the Zairean government to preserve the status quo.

Most Africans accept this as the overriding priority: the continent has enough problems without its constituent states starting to quarrel over their boundaries. There are a few losers from this policy (which has been endorsed by the Organization of African Unity) but they can be counted on the fingers of one hand: the two important ones are Togo (which saw a significant proportion of its nuclear Ewe tribe incorporated in Ghana during the post-First World War division of Togoland), and more notably Somalia. One of the most homogeneous people in Africa, the Somali found themselves at the end of the colonial period living under five different regimes – in French, British and Italian Somaliland, in the Ogaden region of Ethiopia and the Northern Frontier province of Kenya: on independence the Somali republic (ex-British and Italian Somalilands) symbolized its view of Somalia's true extent by placing a five-pointed star on its flag. It is not at all unlikely that French Somaliland will one day opt for union with the Somali republic, but there seems no way that the remaining two Somali-speaking areas can be added to the republic without war. In the Ogaden this began in 1964.

PORTUGAL'S determination to hang on in Africa was sustained through the 1960s by its reactionary old ruler, Salazar. In 1970 (four years after Salazar's death) there was a revolution and a complete about-face. Dismayed by the success of the liberation movements that were already in control of much of the mainland territories, the new Portuguese government decided to pull out entirely and immediately. Three quarters of a million settlers were brought home and during 1974–5 Angola, Mozambique and Portuguese Guinea (as Guinea-Bissau) became sovereign states. (So did the Cape Verde Islands, and São Tomé and Principe.) Angola, initially disputed between three different independence movements, finally fell to a Cuban-backed Marxist group: hardline Marxists also took over in Mozambique.

The Portuguese withdrawal left Rhodesia completely exposed and in 1978 the white settlers there conceded the inevitability of black rule. The changeover, scheduled to take place at the end of the year, was to be marked by the adoption of a new name for the country, Zimbabwe: the question was whether Zimbabwe would be born of this compromise or imposed unilaterally by the guerilla groups operating from Zambia and Mozambique. South Africa, the last bastion of white supremacy, remained utterly intransigent as far as concessions to its black majority were concerned: it did agree to South-West Africa becoming independent (at the end of 1978, under the name Namibia) but most observers suspected that the proposed constitution would enable the white element there (10 per cent of the population) to keep control of the country.

Free Africa also had its disputes. The Spanish had agreed that Morocco and Mauritania could divide the Spanish strip of the Sahara between them: the Algerians bitterly resented this and supported a local independence movement in a guerilla war against the occupying forces. Ethiopia was beset on two sides. The Somalis were gradually conquering the Ogaden, while in Eritrea various liberation movements had gained control over the countryside and only the largest towns remained in Ethiopian hands. But Ethiopia was not finished yet. A military coup in 1974 forced the abdication of the aged emperor, a Marxist group emerged out of the resulting junta and the Russians agreed to support it in an offensive against the Somalis. This succeeded (early 1978) though a similar move in Eritrea petered out (mid-1978). Another country with multiple problems was Chad, which had Libya claiming (and occupying) a strip of her territory in the north and the rest of the Saharan provinces in the hands of the liberation movement of the local Tuareg, the Toubou.

The list of military coups continued to lengthen. In 1971 General Amin took over in Uganda and General Acheampong in Ghana (once again the Ghanaian army promised to restore civilian rule in due course: General Amin disclaimed any such intention): there were other takeovers in Niger, Chad and Mauritania (in 1974, 1975 and 1978 respectively). Places to gain their freedom include the three Moslem islands in the Comoro group, which declared themselves independent in 1975 (the Christian one, Mayotte, refused to go along with them and is currently still a French protectorate), and French Somaliland, which received its freedom in 1977 and took the name of its chief town, Djibouti. Dahomey changed its name to Benin (in 1975: a bit confusing this if you think where the original state of Benin was); the Central African Republic became the Central African Empire in 1977.

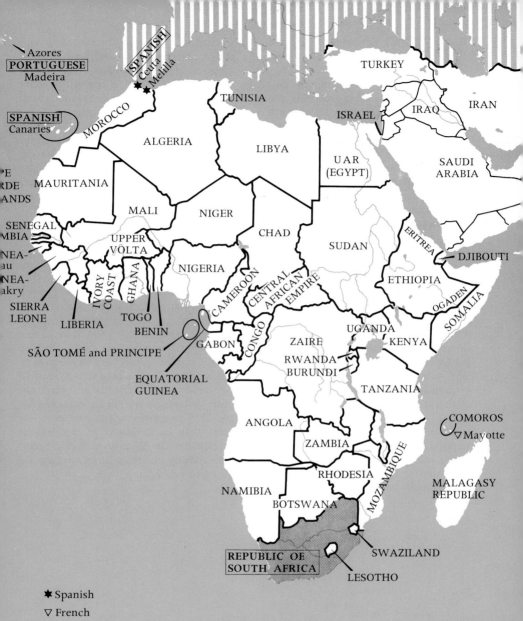

Azores

PORTUGUESE
Madeira

SPANISH
Canaries

SPANISH
Ceuta
Melilla

'E
RDE
ANDS

SENEGAL
MBIA

NEA-
au

NEA-
akry

SIERRA
LEONE

LIBERIA

TOGO

BENIN

SÃO TOMÉ and PRINCIPE

EQUATORIAL
GUINEA

MOROCCO

ALGERIA

TUNISIA

LIBYA

MAURITANIA

MALI

NIGER

UPPER
VOLTA

NIGERIA

IVORY
COAST

GHANA

CAMEROON

GABON

CONGO

CHAD

CENTRAL
AFRICAN
EMPIRE

ZAIRE

RWANDA
BURUNDI

TURKEY

ISRAEL

IRAQ

IRAN

UAR
(EGYPT)

SAUDI
ARABIA

SUDAN

ERITREA

DJIBOUTI

ETHIOPIA

OGADEN

SOMALIA

UGANDA

KENYA

TANZANIA

ANGOLA

ZAMBIA

RHODESIA

NAMIBIA

BOTSWANA

MOZAMBIQUE

COMOROS
▽Mayotte

MALAGASY
REPUBLIC

**REPUBLIC OF
SOUTH AFRICA**

SWAZILAND

LESOTHO

★ Spanish
▽ French

AD **1978**

WHAT happens to the political map of Africa between now and the end of the century is anyone's guess and, of course, there can't be anything certain about any map for the year 2000. However, it is a reasonable prediction that the demographic map will look something like this. It is very similar to the last one dealing with population, the one for AD 1800, except that everything is ten times bigger. This applies not only to the total population, which amounts to 700 million as against seventy million, but to the value of the symbol, ten million as against one. Because of this the two distributions can be directly compared. Doing so shows two areas of disproportionate increase: Egypt, which is in the grip of the sort of population explosion that drives planners to despair, and South Africa, relatively underdeveloped in 1800 but now the continent's most advanced economy. The balancing areas of relatively low growth are the drought-troubled regions of the Sahel and the Horn.

The symbols do not give any indication of ethnic divisions. The most important of these is the split between white and black in South Africa where, on present trends, the end of the century figures will be 6.5 million whites as against thirty-five million blacks, with other groups (coloureds and Asians) amounting to six million. This represents a relative fall in the white share from its present 17 per cent (and a peak of 22 per cent in the first quarter of this century) to 13.5 per cent. It seems a dangerously low figure for an elite trying to keep all the good things to itself. Nonetheless, if they are there at all, the whites are going to be in power and most people think that, barring outside intervention, they will be. Up to AD 2000, that is.

Africa's current rate of population growth is higher than the world average, indeed at near 2.5 per cent per annum, almost twice as high. This means that Africans will make up 12 per cent of the world's population in the year 2000 as against 10 per cent in 1975 and only 7 per cent as recently as 1800. A lot of this is simply ground recovered − before Africa started to fall behind the rest of the world its share was of the order of 10 per cent − but Africans are certainly going to be increasingly important in the world of tomorrow. If the continent has more than its fair share of problems it clearly has the vitality to tackle them. The coming chapters in its history are going to be exciting ones.

130

10 million people

population in
AD 2000

Index

This is basically an index to the text, not to the maps, but for location purposes nearly all the entries for places and peoples start with a map reference. This is printed in bold type.

Occasionally the bold-type entry refers to the subject of a map, not to an item on it. In these cases the word map appears as part of the reference, as for example 'population in AD 200 *map* **36**'.

READ MORE IN PENGUIN

In every corner of the world, on every subject under the sun, Penguin represents quality and variety – the very best in publishing today.

For complete information about books available from Penguin – including Puffins, Penguin Classics and Arkana – and how to order them, write to us at the appropriate address below. Please note that for copyright reasons the selection of books varies from country to country.

In the United Kingdom: Please write to *Dept. JC, Penguin Books Ltd, FREEPOST, West Drayton, Middlesex UB7 0BR*

If you have any difficulty in obtaining a title, please send your order with the correct money, plus ten per cent for postage and packaging, to *PO Box No. 11, West Drayton, Middlesex UB7 0BR*

In the United States: Please write to *Penguin USA Inc., 375 Hudson Street, New York, NY 10014*

In Canada: Please write to *Penguin Books Canada Ltd, 10 Alcorn Avenue, Suite 300, Toronto, Ontario M4V 3B2*

In Australia: Please write to *Penguin Books Australia Ltd, 487 Maroondah Highway, Ringwood, Victoria 3134*

In New Zealand: Please write to *Penguin Books (NZ) Ltd,182–190 Wairau Road, Private Bag, Takapuna, Auckland 9*

In India: Please write to *Penguin Books India Pvt Ltd, 706 Eros Apartments, 56 Nehru Place, New Delhi 110 019*

In the Netherlands: Please write to *Penguin Books Netherlands B.V., Keizersgracht 231 NL–1016 DV Amsterdam*

In Germany: Please write to *Penguin Books Deutschland GmbH, Friedrichstrasse 10–12, W–6000 Frankfurt/Main 1*

In Spain: Please write to *Penguin Books S. A., C. San Bernardo 117–6⁰ E–28015 Madrid*

In Italy: Please write to *Penguin Italia s.r.l., Via Felice Casati 20, I–20124 Milano*

In France: Please write to *Penguin France S. A., 17 rue Lejeune, F–31000 Toulouse*

In Japan: Please write to *Penguin Books Japan, Ishikiribashi Building, 2–5–4, Suido, Tokyo 112*

In Greece: Please write to *Penguin Hellas Ltd, Dimocritou 3, GR–106 71 Athens*

In South Africa: Please write to *Longman Penguin Southern Africa (Pty) Ltd, Private Bag X08, Bertsham 2013*

BY THE SAME AUTHOR

The Penguin Atlas of Ancient History

The Penguin Atlas of Ancient History illustrates in a chronological series of maps, the evolution and flux of races in Europe, the Mediterranean area, and the Near East, from 50,000 B.C. to the fourth century A.D.

The Penguin Atlas of Medieval History

Colin McEvedy's pioneering atlas, revised and expanded for this edition, treats as one unit the Mediterranean, Europe and the nomads' steppeland to the East (the habitat of Huns, Turks and Mongols). Illuminating maps and lively commentaries present the towns and trade routes, the changing population patterns, the boundaries of Christendom (and later Islam) and the ever-shifting political units.

The Penguin Atlas of Recent History

Using the same familiar and highly praised formula of a chronological sequence of maps - in this volume a base map of Europe – Colin McEvedy provides detailed commentary on the political and military developments that can be expressed in geographical terms.

The Penguin Atlas of North American History

In over forty maps and a detailed parallel commentary, Colin McEvedy has compiled an absorbing account of the history of North America. With particular emphasis on the major developments, he traces the evolution of the continent from prehistory through to the Indian settlements, the colonization of the land by Europeans, the expansion of the frontier, the revolution and Civil War that resulted in the acceptance of new states and territories into the Union.

and
The Atlas of World Population History
with Richard Jones